Sew SENSATIONAL *Gifts*

OTHER BOOKS AVAILABLE FROM CHILTON

Robbie Fanning, Series Editor

Contemporary Quilting Series

Contemporary Quilting Techniques, by Pat Cairns

Fast Patch, by Anita Hallock

Fourteen Easy Baby Quilts, by Margaret Dittman

Machine-Quilted Jackets, Vests, and Coats, by Nancy Moore

Picture Quilts, by Carolyn Vosberg Hall

Precision Pieced Quilts Using the Foundation Method, by Jane Hall and Dixie Haywood

The Quilter's Guide to Rotary Cutting, by Donna Poster

Quilts by the Slice, by Beckie Olson

Scrap Quilts Using Fast Patch, by Anita Hallock

Speed-Cut Quilts, by Donna Poster

Super Simple Quilts, by Kathleen Eaton

Teach Yourself Machine Piecing and Quilting, by Debra Wagner

Three-Dimensional Appliqué, by Jodie Davis

Creative Machine Arts Series

ABCs of Serging, by Tammy Young and Lori Bottom

The Button Lover's Book, by Marilyn Green

Claire Shaeffer's Fabric Sewing Guide

The Complete Book of Machine Embroidery, by Robbie and Tony Fanning

Creative Nurseries Illustrated, by Debra Terry and Juli Plooster

Creative Serging Illustrated, by Pati Palmer, Gail Brown, and Sue Green

Distinctive Serger Gifts and Crafts, by Naomi Baker and Tammy Young

The Fabric Lover's Scrapbook, by Margaret Dittman

Friendship Quilts by Hand and Machine, by Carolyn Vosburg Hall

Gifts Galore, by Jane Warnick and Jackie Dodson

How to Make Soft Jewelry, by Jackie Dodson

Innovative Serging, by Gail Brown and Tammy Young

Innovative Sewing, by Gail Brown and Tammy Young

Owner's Guide to Sewing Machines, Sergers, and Knitting Machines, by Gale Grigg Hazen

Petite Pizzazz, by Barb Griffin

Putting on the Glitz, by Sandra L. Hatch and Ann Boyce

Serged Garments in Minutes, by Tammy Young and Naomi Baker

Sew, Serge, Press, by Jan Saunders

Sewing and Collecting Vintage Fashions, by Eileen MacIntosh

Simply Serge Any Fabric, by Naomi Baker and Tammy Young

Soft Gardens: Make Flowers with Your Sewing Machine, by Yvonne Perez-Collins

Twenty Easy Machine-Made Rugs, by Jackie Dodson

Know Your Sewing Machine Series, by Jackie Dodson

Know Your Bernina, second edition

Know Your Brother, with Jane Warnick

Know Your Elna, with Carol Ahles

Know Your New Home, with Judi Cull and Vicki Lyn Hastings

Know Your Pfaff, with Audrey Griese

Know Your Sewing Machine

Know Your Singer

Know Your Viking, with Jan Saunders

Know Your White, with Jan Saunders

Know Your Serger Series, by Naomi Baker and Tammy Young

Know Your baby lock

Know Your Pfaff Hobbylock

Know Your Serger

Know Your White Superlock

Teach Yourself to Sew Better Series, by Jan Saunders

A Step-by-Step Guide to Your Bernina

A Step-by-Step Guide to Your New Home

A Step-by-Step Guide to Your Sewing Machine

A Step-by-Step Guide to Your Viking

Sew SENSATIONAL *Gifts*

NAOMI BAKER
& TAMMY YOUNG

Chilton Book Company
Radnor, Pennsylvania

Published in Radnor, Pennsylvania 19089, by Chilton Book Company

Designed by Anthony Jacobson

Manufactured in the United States of America

Library of Congress Cataloging-in-Publication Data

Baker, Naomi
    Sew sensational gifts / Naomi Baker and Tammy Young.
        p. cm. – (Creative machine arts series)
    Includes index.
    ISBN 0-8019-8237-5 (pbk.)
    1. Sewing. 2. Gifts. I. Young, Tammy. II. Title. III. Series.

TT715.B33 1993

646.2–dc20   92-56584
                                                              CIP

1 2 3 4 5 6 7 8 9 0   2 1 0 9 8 7 6 5 4 3

Contents

Foreword

All of Tammy and Naomi's books are based on the age-old adage of KISS: keep it simple, silly. This book is no different. The easy-to-follow diagrams make each project super-simple, yet they avoid the "loving hands at home" look with the quality of their selections. Now you can make look-alikes to those unaffordable gifts found in specialty gift shops. These are truly useful gift ideas that will be appreciated by the receiver, not junk to be relegated to Goodwill.

As usual, Chris Hansen's illustrations are outstanding. You will have no trouble following the clear instructions. The authors have given you all the patterns, measurements, and supply lists. You merely select the colors you prefer to use and head for your trusty machine.

My favorite is the fold-up pillow comforter. It's a must for anyone living in chilly climates or for college-bound students. The bulletin board would also be excellent for any kid's bedroom.

This book is not just for adults. It would be a good way both to help kids make great handmade gifts and to learn some basic sewing skills—like putting a zipper in an Ultrasuede shoe bag. I wish I'd had this book when I was 10 years old.

Clotilde, President
Clotilde, Inc.

Preface

We know you'll enjoy the satisfaction of making and giving truly novel gifts with handcrafted charm. In this hurry-up world, the fact that you took the time to make a special gift for someone says you really care. And it's always nice to know that most of your recipients will consider your gift a treasured keepsake.

Much of the feedback we've received from our previous books is praise for the easy-to-follow projects that we incorporated. With that in mind, we decided to write a book on gift projects, including both sewing and serging ideas, duplicating many of the novelty items found at retail stores and from numerous mail-order sources.

For those who don't own a serger, the step-by-step project instructions can all be accomplished with the sewing machine. But speedy serging tips are included throughout the book to allow those with these machines to choose the construction method they prefer.

Following most of the projects are decorative options, giving you the inspiration to go beyond the basic project instructions and add special touches to make your own unique creations.

This book is organized by recipient or special gift type. We've included projects for infants and children, brides, women, and men. Also featured are gifts for the home and patio, country-oriented gift ideas, special items for the bath and boudoir, and useful presents that busy people can use outside the home.

In a hurry? Each gift chapter begins with a quick and easy project—one that's perfect for a last-minute gift. Then the remaining projects progress from the least complicated to the most advanced or time-consuming. But none of the projects are too difficult for someone with the knowledge of basic sewing skills.

In addition, we've included an overview of basic sewing techniques and information in Chapter 1 and some fun wrapping ideas in Chapter 10.

We selected the projects in this book based on our own taste, not including any that we wouldn't be proud to give ourselves. We also tried to choose items for which instructions are not readily available to home-sewers.

Although a few of the projects require special materials, all can be found in well-stocked fabric stores or through the mail-order sources listed in the back of this book. Many of the projects can be made with scraps you already have on hand.

So get right to it, delight your friends and yourself, and have fun sewing sensational gifts!

Naomi Baker and Tammy Young

Acknowledgments

A special thank you to all of the sewing enthusiasts who have read and appreciated our previous books. We wouldn't continue to write more, including this one, without all of the wonderful encouragement and support.

Comments such as "Thanks for providing such wonderful inspiration through your books," "I am delighted with the information in the book," and "It's easy to read, understand, and use. Thank you for writing such a concise and informative book" keep us pushing ourselves to work longer hours, temporarily neglect families and friends, and put off everything else that can wait until a later day.

We've also valued suggestions and ideas readers have given us about the content and direction of our books. "Give us more great projects," "Stick to the basics—don't make things too complicated," and simply "Continue to write more of the same" are the type of observations that let us know what people are looking for. We love to hear from and talk to as many readers as possible.

Thanks also to our talented production team:

Chris Hansen, illustrations—His delightful detailed line drawings, technical expertise, and friendship are invaluable.

Christopher J. Kuppig, Chilton General Manager—Under his leadership, the company is making major contributions in the area of sewing and craft publishing, and we're proud to be associated with them.

Robbie Fanning, Chilton Series Editor—We very much appreciate her encouragement, understanding, efficiency, and wealth of knowledge in all facets of sewing.

Kathryn Conover, Chilton Senior Editor—Kathy not only has a focused understanding of what is needed for a successful book but also has the talent, patience, and detail orientation to steamroll it through.

Anthony Jacobson, Chilton artist and designer—In addition to his capable book and cover design and photography supervision, Tony is a pleasure to work with.

Jeanine LaBorne, Chilton Sales Manager, Specialty Markets—We wouldn't continue to write so many books if they weren't selling. She tirelessly makes sure they're out there where people can find them.

Nancy Ellis, Chilton Publicity/Promotions/Advertising Manager—Even as a brand-new first-time mother, her professionalism and hard work shine through.

Susan Clarey, Chilton Acquisitions Editor—She makes sure we continue to get assignments and has infinite patience when we keep changing our minds about what we want to write next.

Cate Keller Lowe, typesetting and layout—Somehow she makes everything fit and at the same time focuses unerringly on all of the intricate details to get the book ready for the printer.

The following are registered trademark names used in this book: *Lycra, Ribbon Floss, Teflon, Ultrasuede,* and *Velcro.*

CHAPTER ONE
Basic Giftmaking

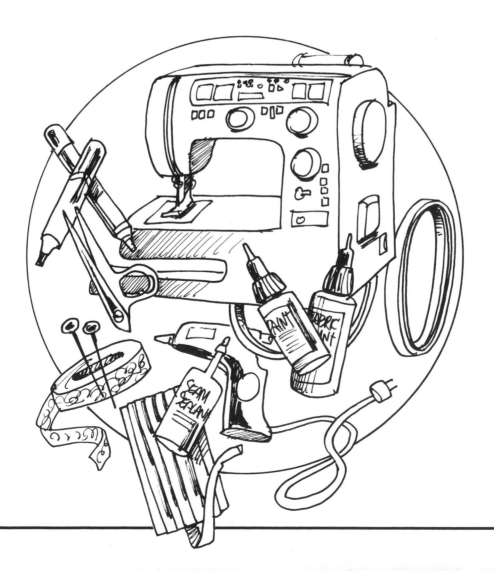

Fig. 1-1 This book lets you choose projects from fast and easy to more involved.

All of the projects in this book are relatively easy if you know a few elementary sewing skills. The instructions range from super simple and effortless to more time-consuming and elaborate. Choose the ones you'll make based on the recipient or occasion and the amount of time you have available. (Fig. 1-1)

In this chapter, we'll review some helpful tips and techniques that apply to many of the projects we've included. If you're unsure of a sewing-related term that we've used anywhere in the book, refer to the Glossary of Sewing Terms beginning on page 143.

Enlarging Patterns

Although you won't need to purchase additional sewing patterns to complete the projects in this book, you will often need to enlarge the pattern grids or layouts illustrated. The easiest enlargement method is to take the book to a commercial photocopying business. They usually have enlargement capabilities—just explain the scale to the machine operator.

Another relatively easy method of enlarging our patterns is to use pattern tracing paper with a 1"-square grid. Transfer the pattern outline and markings onto the grid paper, square-by-square, to enlarge it proportionately. (Fig. 1-2)

Gluing Pointers

Many of the projects in this book call for some type of glue. In general, we recommend glue stick for glue-basting, when you want to position fabric or

trim temporarily so that it can be stitched over accurately later. Glue stick is widely available under a variety of brand names.

We used a glue gun for permanent gluing in most projects. Originally available only as a "hot glue gun," this handy tool melts sticks of special glue and releases a fine line of it when you squeeze the trigger. Now glue guns are available in lower temperatures, too, so you have less chance of getting burned by the hot liquid. Work slowly and methodically to avoid drips and glue tails.

A myriad of other glues is now on the market and many of them give good results. If you prefer using a fabric or craft glue instead of a glue gun, be sure to test first to see if the product will hold during use.

Fast Fabric Painting

Using fabric paints is a speedy option for decorating your gift projects. Becoming skilled with this medium does take a little practice but can be lots of fun.

Follow the manufacturer's instructions and a few simple guidelines when using fabric paint:

♦ If the finished project will be washable, prewash the fabric before painting on it.

♦ Don't use fabric paint on a project that will need to be dry cleaned unless the brand is specifically labeled dry-cleanable.

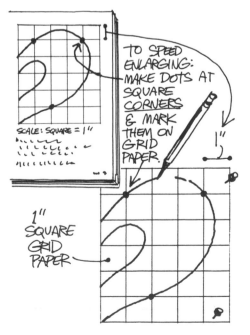

Fig. 1-2 Use the scale given on each grid or layout to make a full-size pattern.

♦ Put freezer paper or cardboard on the underside of the fabric you are painting in case the paint bleeds through.

♦ Scrape away any mistakes with the blade of a butter knife or the edge of a credit card. Remove the remaining paint with a damp cotton swab.

♦ Let the paint dry at least 72 hours before using or washing the project it is on.

Practice on fabric scraps before beginning your project. Simple designs are usually the best choice. Bottles with fine or "writer" tips are the easiest to control. Paints labeled "dimensional" are used for outlining.

With the cap on, shake the bottle vigorously toward the tip to mix the paint and remove any air bubbles. Remove the cap and place the bottle tip on the fabric. Hold the bottle at a 45-degree angle like a pencil. (Fig. 1-3)

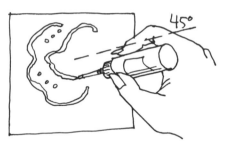

Fig. 1-3 Practice with fabric paint before working on the project.

Squeeze the bottle gently to begin painting. Move your hand slowly and evenly. Stop periodically, put the cap back on, and shake the bottle toward the tip again. To avoid smearing your work, begin at the upper left (if you're right-handed) and work down and across. If you're left-handed, begin at the upper right.

Easy Appliquéing

Many of the projects throughout this book include appliqués. In other projects, we suggest that you use them as a decorative option.

For the simplest appliqué method, use a paper-backed fusible web:

1. Trace or draw the appliqué design on the paper side of the web.

2. Fuse the web to the wrong side of the appliqué fabric and let it cool. (Fig. 1-4)

3. Cut out the appliqué following the traced outline.

4. Peel the paper backing off the appliqué, position the design on the project, and fuse it in place.

5. Hide the raw edges of the fused appliqué using a satin-length zigzag stitch or cover them with dimensional fabric paint using the previous techniques.

Machine Embroidery and Monogramming

As you're making special gifts for friends or relatives, you have an excellent opportunity to get the most out of your sewing machine. Most of today's computerized models have lettering capabilities. If yours does, program it to sew a monogram or name to personalize many of the gifts in this book. Some machines have other decorative options as well. Even the simplest decorative stitch can add interest and make your gift unique.

If you don't have programming capabilities, you can still embroider using free-machine embroidery with the presser foot removed and the feed dogs lowered or covered. If you haven't tried it, this technique takes a little practice, but you may enjoy it so much that you'll become an enthusiast.

Fig. 1-4 Finish the appliqué edges with either a satin-length zigzag stitch or fabric paint.

Whether you're embroidering with programmed machine stitches or using the free-machine method, it helps to stabilize the fabric in an embroidery hoop designed specifically for machine embroidery. (Fig. 1-5)

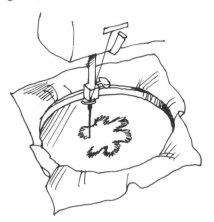

Fig. 1-5 Remove the presser foot and lower or cover the feed dogs for free-machine embroidery.

Follow these general tips for successful machine embroidery:

♦ An open-toed embroidery foot gives better visibility on machine embroidery, but a regular embroidery foot will hold the fabric more securely. The foot should have a scoop on the underside to allow it to climb easily over the build-up of the thread.

♦ Use the smallest size of needle for your machine that won't cause skipped stitches and matches the thickness of the thread. Always begin with a sharp new needle.

♦ Stitch slowly to reduce puckering and skipped stitches.

♦ Stabilize the underside of the fabric if you are having problems with tunneling and puckering. Use interfacing, tear-away stabilizer, or paper.

♦ Loosen the machine's upper and lower tensions as necessary to perfect the stitch.

Before you begin working on your project, test first using the same design and thread on scraps of the project fabric.

Smart Stuffing

In most cases we recommend polyester fiberfill for stuffing pillows and other projects because it's washable, handles well, and doesn't get lumpy. If you are putting stuffing into hard-to-reach areas such as corners, curves, or small spaces, use a screwdriver

or a stuffing tool to ensure the fiberfill is distributed evenly. Be sure to stuff firmly. It always takes a lot more stuffing than you'd expect.

Helpful Sewing Basics

When we completed the projects in this book, we found that several of the same techniques were used in many of them. Here's a quick review:

Double hem—press a narrow hem to the wrong side and edge-stitch or top-stitch it in place. Press an equal amount to the wrong side again, enclosing the raw edge. Edge-stitch if the hem is only 1/8" deep, or top-stitch near the hem edge if it is wider. (Double hems are usually not wider than 1/2".) (Fig. 1-6)

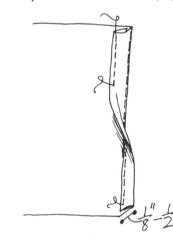

Fig. 1-6 Press and stitch the fabric to the wrong side twice to create a double hem.

French seam—stitch a narrow seam first with the fabric wrong sides together, and trim the allowances to about 1/8". Wrap the fabric right sides together around the allowances and stitch again, enclosing the allowances on the wrong side of the fabric. Most French seams are 1/4"-wide or less. (Fig. 1-7)

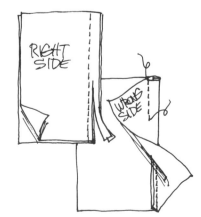

Fig. 1-7 Stitch a French seam twice, enclosing the raw edges.

Binding—vary the techniques used depending on whether you are using a bias strip or a finished-edge ribbon to bind an edge.

Two-step method using bias tape or a bias strip: Match one long raw edge of the bias tape or bias strip, right sides together, to the edge of the fabric. Sew or serge a narrow seam (on the bias tape or on a prefolded bias strip, position the fold on the seamline). (Fig. 1-8)

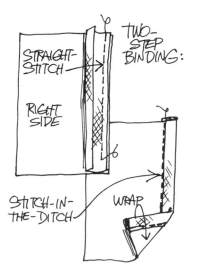

Fig. 1-8 Use bias tape or a prefolded bias strip to bind an edge easily.

Then wrap the bias around the seam allowances to the wrong side and stitch-in-the-ditch to secure it. You have several options at this point:

♦ Wrap the binding around the edge as snugly as possible. Stitch-in-the-ditch from the right side to catch the folded edge on the underside. (Fig. 1-9)

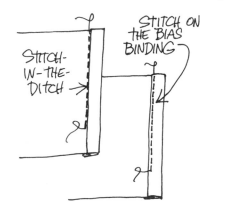

Fig. 1-9 Position the top-stitching to catch the folded edge underneath.

♦ To vary the look, you may choose to stitch on the binding, next to the seamline, catching the fold on the underside.

♦ If the bias strip has not been prefolded, either turn the edge under now, serge-finish it, or leave it raw and trim the excess (if the underside will not be exposed). Stitch-in-the-ditch or on the binding to secure the underside. (Fig. 1-10)

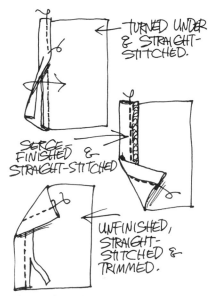

Fig. 1-10 Choose from three options when you bind an edge with an unfolded bias strip.

One-step method using ribbon as the binding: Press the ribbon in half lengthwise. Place the ribbon on the project edge, with its raw edges against the ribbon's inside foldline. Top-stitch along the upper edge of the ribbon, being sure to catch the ribbon's under edge in the stitching. (Fig. 1-11)

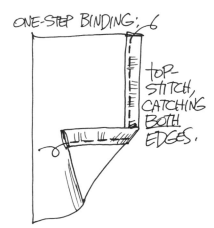

Fig. 1-11 Fold grosgrain or satin ribbon over the fabric edge to bind it.

Ending the binding: When the binding end will be exposed at the edge of a project, turn the raw edge under before stitching over it. If the edge being bound is circular, turn under the binding end that will be exposed on top of the finished project. (Fig. 1-12)

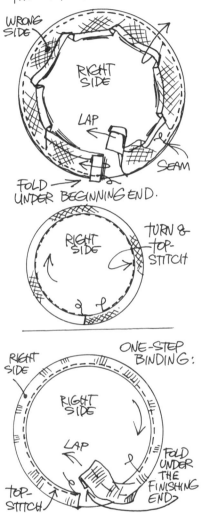

Fig. 1-12 On two-step binding, fold under the beginning end before seaming. Fold under the finishing end on one-step binding.

Piping–purchase piping or make it by wrapping a bias strip snugly over cording and stitching next to the cording edge using a zipper foot. Apply piping to a seamline by sewing it, over the original stitching, to the right side of one fabric layer with cut edges matching. Align the second layer of fabric on top, right sides together, sandwiching the piping in between. Sew again over the original stitching lines so the finished piping is positioned on the right side of the project. (Fig. 1-13)

Serging Techniques

Throughout this book, we have given optional serging instructions for many of the projects. There are many more decorative serging options that we didn't have room to cover in this book. For additional decorative serging ideas and instructions, refer to the "Know Your Serger" series listed under Other Books by the Authors on page 146.

Materials Needed

For every project in this book, we have listed the supplies you'll need. You will probably have many of them on hand. We do recommend using fabric scraps and material from your fabric stash whenever possible. Making gifts is a great way use up fabric you wouldn't be caught dead in (and a great excuse to buy more fabric)!

When a specialty thread is recommended, such as machine-embroidery thread or pearl cotton, we list it in the project. But we assume you will have matching or coordinating all-purpose thread available for each project as well, so we have not listed it every time.

Most supplies can be found at your local fabric store or sewing-machine dealer. However, if you are having trouble finding specific items in your location, refer to Mail-order Resources beginning on page 145.

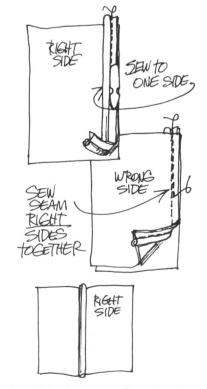

Fig. 1-13 Sew piping into a seamline using two steps.

CHAPTER TWO
Gifts for Babies and Children

BEGINNER BALL

Baby is never too young to appreciate a ball—who knows, he or she might be a future star athlete! Although this ball doesn't bounce, it's a tactile treat and easily held by any infant. Use fabric scraps with lots of contrast for the most interest to the baby. At this age, their eyes see the greatest contrasts (such as black and white) the most vividly. (Fig. 2-1)

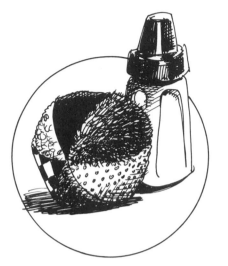

Fig. 2-1 Make a multitextured ball with a rattle inside to delight any infant. It's machine washable, too.

Materials Needed

♦ Remnants of six different washable fabrics with varied textures and colors, such as gripper fabric, terry, velour, nylon/*Lycra*, synthetic furs, or *Ultrasuede*

♦ One large handful of polyester fiberfill

♦ Small pill or film container

♦ Dried beans (approximately 12)

Cutting Directions

♦ Cut one ball section from each of the six fabrics, using the pattern grid. (Fig. 2-2)

How-Tos

Sew or serge all seams using 1/4" allowances.

1. Sew the ball sections together, matching the dots and cut edges. Sew from dot to dot. Leave 3" of one section open for turning and stuffing. Turn the ball right side out. (Fig. 2-3)

2. Place the beans in the container and close tightly. Glue the lid on, if necessary.

3. Lightly stuff the ball, positioning the container in the center with fiberfill around it. Adjust the stuffing so the container is completely covered. Add additional stuffing to fill the ball. Hand-sew the opening closed.

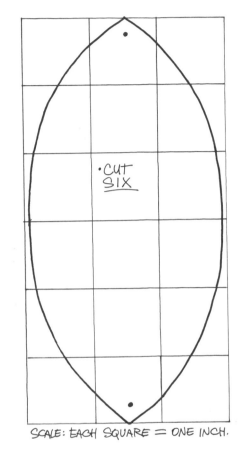

SCALE: EACH SQUARE = ONE INCH.

Fig. 2-2 Cut each ball section from a different texture of fabric.

Fig. 2-3 Sew the sections together from dot to dot, leaving an opening on one of the seams.

Decorative Options

♦ Machine-embroider the date and baby's name (or your own) on a satin ribbon. Insert the ribbon ends into a seamline near the top of the ball.

♦ Add interest to some of the fabric sections by applying machine embroidery or decorative serging before cutting out and sewing the ball.

SPILL-CATCHER MATS

Give a gift that keeps floors and car seats neat and tidy under a busy little one. The clear vinyl quickly wipes clean of any spills or messes. With an easy self-binding, the finished high chair mat is 42" square and the car seat mat is 28" by 56". (Fig. 2-4)

Fig. 2-4 Use markers, craft paint, or ornaments to decorate a spill-catcher mat.

Materials Needed

(High chair mat yardage is listed first with car mat yardage in parentheses.)

♦ 1-1/6 yard (7/8 yard) 60"-wide heavy clear vinyl

♦ 1-1/4 yard (7/8 yard) 60"-wide mediumweight water-repellent fabric like nylon pack cloth. When using decorative options (see page 10), select a solid-color fabric so that the embellished design will be more visible.

Cutting Directions

♦ Cut a 42" vinyl square and a 44" fabric square for the floor mat.

♦ Cut a 28" by 56" vinyl rectangle and a 30" by 58" fabric rectangle for the car mat.

How-Tos

For all stitching, use a long stitch length. We recommend using clothespins instead of pinning. If you prefer pins, use them on the fabric only—they'll leave holes in the vinyl.

1. For an optional painted design (see Decorative Options following this project), place the vinyl over a design and trace-paint on the vinyl 3" from the outer edge. Allow the paint to dry completely before completing the mat.

2. Lightly press 1" of the fabric to the wrong side on all four edges.

3. When encasing ornaments as a decorative option, glue-baste the ornaments to the wrong side of the fabric, approximately 3" from the folded-back cut edges. Allow the glue to dry before completing the mat.

4. Center the vinyl (with the painted side down, if you painted it) on the wrong side of the fabric. Lightly steam above the vinyl to "baste" it into position. (Fig. 2-5)

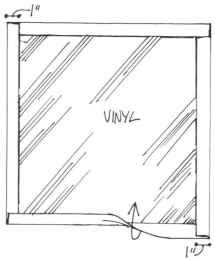

Fig. 2-5 Press 1" of fabric to the wrong side. Then center the vinyl on the wrong side of the fabric.

5. To secure the ornaments, sew around each from the fabric side, a presser foot's distance away. You'll be able to see their outline. (Fig. 2-6)

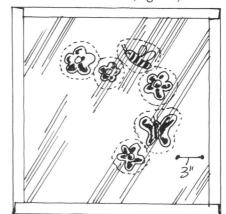

Fig. 2-6 Glue-baste ornaments between the fabric and vinyl before sewing around each one from the underside (fabric side) of the mat.

6. On a flat surface, flatten the vinyl to the fabric. Fold and pin a double hem of the fabric over the vinyl, folding the corners as shown. (Fig. 2-7)

7. Straight-stitch close to the inside hem edge, stitching a rectangle in each corner for extra security.

Decorative Options

♦ Add a painted design using bright-colored permanent markers or fabric paint. If you paint numbers or letters, be sure they're reversed.

♦ Encase flat bright ornaments between the vinyl and fabric when constructing the mat. Use animal shapes, numbers, or letters for an educational impact.

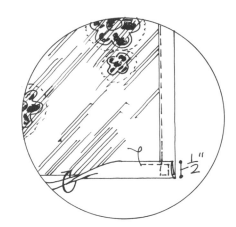

Fig. 2-7 Fold the 1" hem allowance double and straight-stitch the hem, reinforcing the corners.

SOFT 'N' COZY SLIPPERS

Little feet will appreciate these snuggly washable fleece slippers on cold winter nights. They're fast and easy to make—a good place to use scraps you have on hand. The slippers will stretch as the feet grow, but make them with plenty of ease now. The ribbed cuff will hold them on comfortably. (Fig. 2-8)

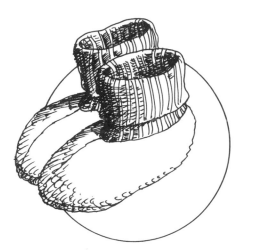

Fig. 2-8 Sew or serge a pair of warm slippers to fit any foot size.

Materials Needed

♦ 1/4 yard (or remnants) of polar fleece

♦ 10" of ribbing

♦ 1/4 yard (or remnants) of rubber gripper fabric or dimensional fabric paint

Cutting Directions

♦ Measure the length of the child's foot and compare it to the length of the sole on the pattern. Allow 1" of ease at the toe and an extra 1/4" for seam allowances. (Enlarge the pattern proportionally for older children or adults.)

♦ Cut two slipper tops and two soles from the fleece. If using gripper fabric, also cut two soles with the fabric on the bias. (Fig. 2-9)

♦ Cut two 7" by 10" cuffs from the ribbing with the greatest stretch in the 7" direction.

How-Tos

Sew or serge using 1/4" seam allowances.

1. With right sides together, sew the center front seams on the slipper tops.

2. If you're using the gripper fabric, place the wrong side of the gripper sole on the right side of the polar fleece sole and treat it as one piece. Matching the center fronts and backs and with right sides together, sew the sole to the lower edge of the slipper top. (Fig. 2-10)

3. Fold the ribbing cuffs in half, right sides together, with the long edges matching and sew them into circles. Finger-press the seam open and fold the circles in half, wrong sides together, to form the cuffs. Mark a position on the cut edges equidistant to the seam.

4. With right sides together and the ribbing on top, match the ribbing seam to the center back mark on the top edge of the slipper and match the ribbing mark to the slipper top center front seam. Sew the cuffs to the slipper, stretching the ribbing to fit. (Fig. 2-11)

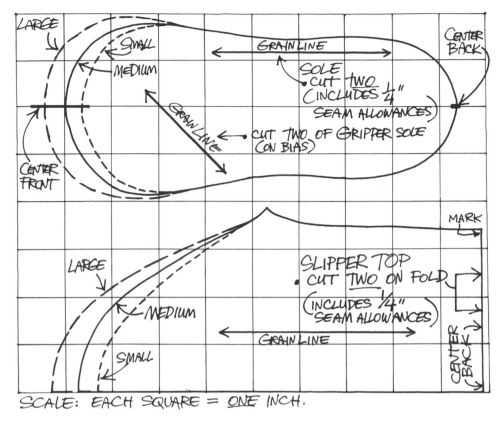

LARGE
SMALL
MEDIUM
CENTER BACK
GRAINLINE
GRAINLINE
SOLE
CUT TWO
(INCLUDES 1/4"
SEAM ALLOWANCES)
CUT TWO OF GRIPPER SOLE
(ON BIAS)
CENTER FRONT
MARK
LARGE
MEDIUM
SMALL
SLIPPER TOP
CUT TWO ON FOLD
(INCLUDES 1/4"
SEAM ALLOWANCES)
GRAINLINE
CENTER BACK

SCALE: EACH SQUARE = ONE INCH.

Fig. 2-9 Measure and adjust the pattern before cutting.

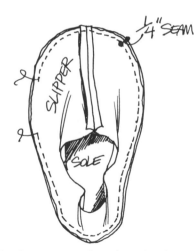

1/4" SEAM
SLIPPER
SOLE

Fig. 2-10 Sew or serge the sole to the slipper.

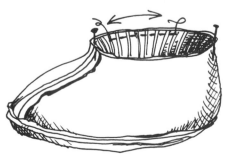

Fig. 2-11 Stretch the ribbing to fit as you sew it to the top of the slipper.

5. Turn the slippers right side out.

6. If you're using dimensional fabric paint instead of the gripper fabric, add squiggles of paint to the soles of the slippers (following the manufacturer's instructions) and let it dry completely.

Decorative Options

♦ Feminize the slippers by sewing a bow where the front seam joins the ribbing. Use your serger to lettuce the folded edge of the ribbing.

♦ Use fabric paint to add a name, initials, or another embellishment to the fleece portion of the slippers.

WRAPPED TO GO

Keep a special infant warm and comfy in this handy baby wrap. With fleece on the outside and cotton interlock or stretch terry on the inside, it washes beautifully. The body-conforming design fits easily into a stroller or car seat. Use binding or decorative serging with optional lace or eyelet trim to personalize the design. (Fig. 2-12)

Fig. 2-12 Feet, a hood, and a quick *Velcro* closure keep baby bundled up and draft-free.

Materials Needed

♦ One yard of stretch fleece for the outer layer

♦ 1-1/8 yards of cotton interlock or stretch terry for the lining and binding

♦ One 1-1/2" square of *Velcro*

Cutting Directions

♦ Using the pattern grid, cut one wrap, one front hood, and two feet sections from both the fleece and the lining. (Fig. 2-13)

♦ Cut three 1-1/4"-wide strips of the interlock with the greatest stretch running the length of the strip. Piece the strips together to form one long strip.

How-Tos

To apply the binding, sew or serge using 1/4" seam allowances.

1. On the separate feet sections, position the fleece and lining right sides together and seam the straight upper edge. Turn right side out and top-stitch the

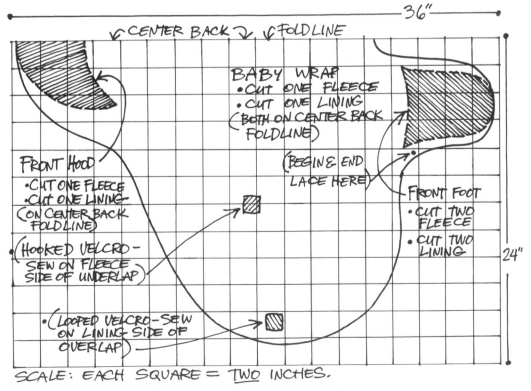

Fig. 2-13 Cut out the wrap, feet sections, and hood from both the fleece and the lining.

seam. Repeat for the lower edge of the separate hood section.

2. To apply the binding, place the wrong sides of the fleece and lining together. Position the separate feet and hood sections with the fleece right sides together at the corresponding positions on the wrap. (The hood and feet will not lie flat.) Beginning on the inside of one foot section, bind the outside edges. (Fig. 2-14)

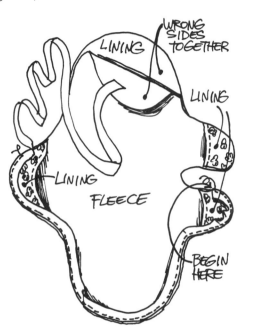

Fig. 2-14 Bind the entire outer edge, attaching the feet and the hood.

Serger tip: Decoratively serge-finish all edges, wrong sides together, attaching the feet and hood sections and eliminating the binding. Use decorative thread in both loopers and a wide, short, balanced 3-thread stitch. You'll need two spools of matching decorative thread, such as crochet thread, pearl cotton, or rayon.

3. Turn the hood and feet right side out. Slightly round the corners of the *Velcro* square and top-stitch one section to each side at the position shown on the grid.

Decorative Options

♦ To add a feminine touch, purchase 4 yards of soft lace or eyelet trim for insertion between the binding and the outer wrap layer.

1. Complete step 1 on page 12.

2. With the right sides of the wrap together, cut edges to match and sandwich the feet and hood

sections between the lining and fleece with the lace positioned between the right sides of the fleece. Begin and end at the dots on the outside foot seams, angling the trim toward the seamline to hide the raw ends. (There will be no trim around the feet sections.) Serge or sew around the wrap, leaving an opening for turning. (Fig. 2-15)

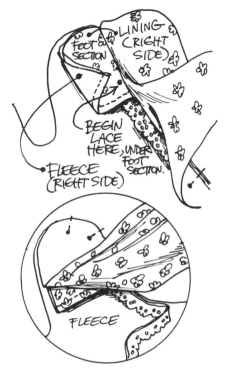

Fig. 2-15 Sandwich lace or eyelet with the wrap right sides together. Turn after seaming.

3. Turn the wrap right side out and top-stitch around the entire edge. (Fig. 2-16)

4. Complete the previous step 3.

♦ Decoratively serge-finish the wrap edges instead of applying binding.

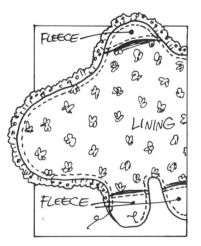

Fig. 2-16 Top-stitch around the outer edge with the lace or eyelet protruding.

MR. TOM—THE FAT CAT

Your favorite budding artist will love this charming muslin cat (featured on the book cover). Make it with permanently marked outlines and let the recipient add the colored details with washable markers. Just toss it into the washer any time it's dirty or whenever you want to create a clean palette—then it's ready to color again. (Fig. 2-17)

Materials Needed

♦ 1/2 yard of unbleached muslin

♦ Polyester fiberfill

♦ One black fine-point permanent marker

♦ One set of nontoxic washable markers

Cutting Directions

Cut two cat shapes, using the pattern grid. (Fig. 2-18)

How-Tos

When sewing, use a 1/4" seam allowance and a short stitch length.

Fig. 2-17 Follow our pattern to make an adorable Mr. Tom or change the permanent markings to create another personality.

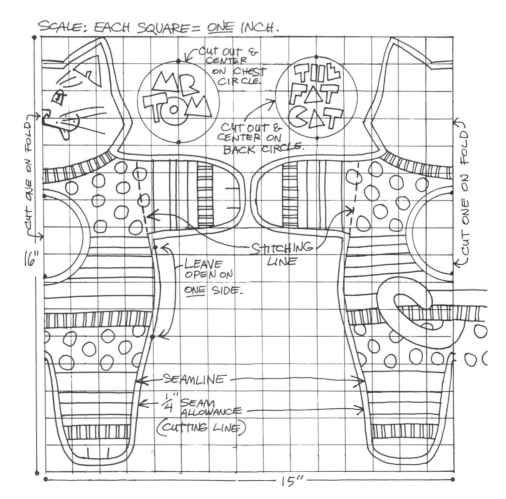

Fig. 2-18 Cut out both cat sections and transfer the markings for the front and back.

1. Transfer the pattern markings in Fig. 2-18 to the two cat shapes using a permanent marker, creating the front and back of the cat. For ease in drawing exact markings, enlarge the pattern grid to full size on a photocopy machine.

2. With right sides together, sew around the cat, leaving the 3" opening on one side for stuffing.

3. Turn the cat right side out and stuff the arms with fiberfill. Straight-stitch from the shoulders to the underarms as marked on the pattern grid. Stuff the ears and head, making sure to fill all the curves completely. Fill the remainder of the cat, stuffing the legs and stomach tightly. Hand-sew the opening closed.

4. Color the cat with watercolor markers, if desired, or save this step for the recipient and include the set of markers as part of the gift. **Note:** Watercolor markers can be as messy as paints but will wash off of skin and clothing with warm soapy water.

Decorative Options

♦ Change the permanent-marker design to create a feminine cat. Tie a ribbon and bow at the neck and add a touch of lace, a strand of pearls or cross-locked beads, and ribbon rosebuds.

♦ Personalize any gender cat by adding the child's name (for example, "Cathy's Cat" in place of "The Fat Cat").

UP-UP-AND-AWAY BIB

Brighten baby's day with this colorful bib featuring corded-edge balloons and a play toy. It's both fun and practical with an easy Velcro closure. To wash, just unsnap the toy ring and toss the bib into the machine. (Fig. 2-19)

Fig. 2-19 Three fabric balloons fly from a plastic play toy on this charming bib.

Materials Needed

♦ 1/2 yard (or a 14" by 16" remnant) of double-sided quilted fabric

♦ Three 4" squares of woven cotton remnants in bright contrasting colored fabrics for the balloon appliqués

♦ One package of double-fold bias binding

♦ 3-1/2" of 1-1/2"-wide *Velcro*

♦ All-purpose thread to match or coordinate with each balloon appliqué fabric

♦ Matching crochet thread or pearl cotton for cording the edges of each balloon appliqué

♦ 6" of snap tape, with a 2" snap spacing

♦ Baby ring toy with brightly colored ornaments, such as circles or keys

♦ Seam sealant

Cutting Directions

♦ Cut one bib from the quilted fabric, using the pattern grid. (Fig. 2-20)

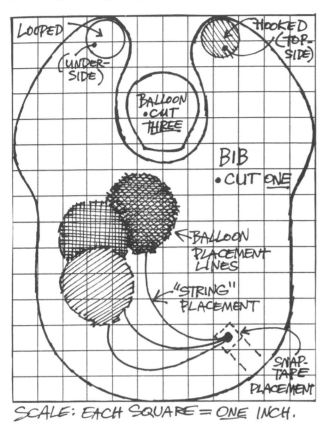

SCALE: EACH SQUARE = ONE INCH.

Fig. 2-20 Cut the bib from quilted fabric and each of the three balloons from bright remnants.

♦ Cut one balloon from each of the three fabric remnants.

♦ Cut two 1-1/2" circles from the *Velcro*.

How-Tos

1. From the wrong side of each balloon, zigzag over the cording around the balloon edge. To begin easily, zigzag several stitches over the cording before inserting the fabric wrong side up. Use a medium length and width zigzag, with one side of the stitches going slightly off the fabric edge. Dab the ends with seam sealant and clip when dry. (Fig. 2-21)

2. Adjust to a slightly wider zigzag with a shorter stitch length. From the right side of the balloon, zigzag over the previous stitching at the lower edge and for 3/4" up each side. (Fig. 2-22)

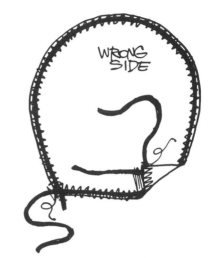

Fig. 2-21 Zigzag over cording on the wrong side of the balloon edges.

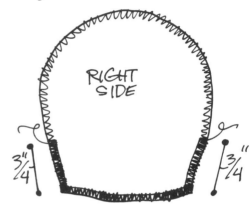

Fig. 2-22 Using a short stitch length, zigzag the balloon bottom from the right side.

> **Serger tip:** Quickly finish the balloon edges in one step using a serged rolled edge instead of the zigzagged cording. After completing step 3, top-stitch the balloons to the bib in step 4.

3. Gather the bottom of the balloons 1/2" from the lower edge by zigzagging over another piece of cording on the wrong side of the fabric. Use a long stitch, being careful not to catch the cording in the stitching.

4. Pin the wrong side of the balloons to the right side of the bib at the placement marks. Gather the lower edges, using the cording. Zigzag over the gathers with a short stitch. Clip the cording ends. Zigzag around the tops of each balloon to secure them to the bib. (Fig. 2-23)

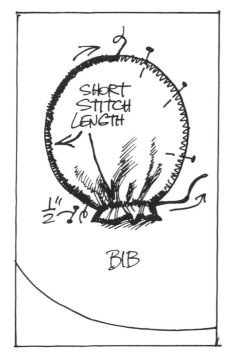

Fig. 2-23 After gathering and zigzagging over the balloon bottom, zigzag around the top edges to attach the balloon to the bib.

5. Use a satin-length zigzag to make balloon strings as shown on the grid.

6. Cut a section of snap tape with at least 3/4" of tape on one side of the snap and 2" on the other. On the ball side of the tape, fold the short end to the wrong side and top-stitch it to the bib, as shown. You may need to use a zipper foot. Finish the shorter end of the opposite side with a narrow double hem. Sew together the remaining cut edges of the tape using a narrow French seam. (Fig. 2-24)

7. Sew the *Velcro* circles to the back of the bib with the hook section on top of the fabric on the right-hand side of the bib and the looped section on the opposite underside. (Fig. 2-25)

8. Bind the bib edge. Thread the ring toy onto the tape and snap it closed.

Serger tip: Decoratively serge-finish the edge, eliminating the binding. Use decorative thread in both loopers and serge-finish using a wide, short, balanced 3-thread stitch. You'll need two spools of matching decorative thread, such as crochet thread or pearl cotton.

Decorative Options

♦ Choose any appliqué design, as long as the materials are washable.

♦ Serge-finish the appliqué edges instead of using a corded zigzag.

♦ Decoratively serge-finish the bib edges instead of applying binding.

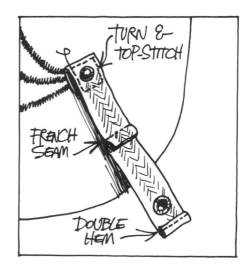

Fig. 2-24 Make a play-toy holder at the end of the balloon strings using snap tape.

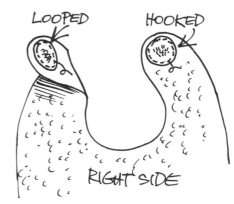

Fig. 2-25 Top-stitch the 1-1/2" *Velcro* circles to the neckline of the bib.

QUILTED NURSERY CADDY

There's a place for everything from lotion to diapers in this handy organizer. Snap or button it to a crib or changing table to store all of baby's essentials conveniently. The Velcro *strip at the bottom hangs any* Velcro-*closure garments close at hand—a good spot for air drying, too. When baby's older, use the caddy as a closet organizer. (Fig. 2-26)*

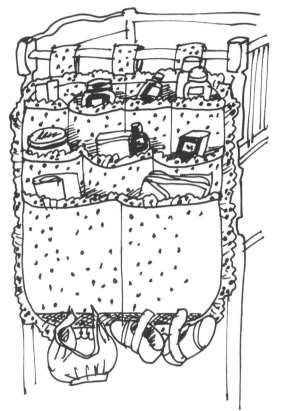

Fig. 2-26 Quickly serge or sew a handy nursery organizer.

Materials Needed

♦ 2/3 yard of quilted fabric

♦ 2/3 yard of coordinating fabric

♦ 2-1/3 yards of 1"-wide ruffled eyelet trim

♦ 1-1/2 yards of 3/4"-wide ruffled eyelet trim

♦ Two 3/4" snaps or buttons

♦ 18" of 1-1/2"-wide *Velcro*

Cutting Directions

♦ Cut an 18" by 21" rectangle from both the quilted and the coordinating fabric.

♦ Cut three 2-1/2" by 16" strips from the quilted fabric.

♦ From the remaining coordinating fabric, cut Pocket One 8-1/2" by 18", Pocket Two 6-1/2" by 18", and Pocket Three 22-1/2" by 18".

How-Tos

Sew or serge using 1/4" seam allowances.

1. Press all three pocket sections in half lengthwise with wrong sides together. Lap the folded edge of each pocket over the right side of the narrower eyelet trim and top-stitch using either a straight-stitch or a delicate decorative stitch. (Fig. 2-27)

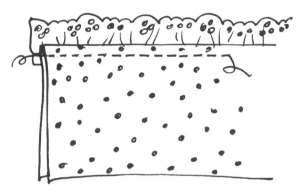

Fig. 2-27 Decorate the pockets by folding them in half and top-stitching ruffled eyelet to the folded edge.

Serger tip: Decoratively serge-finish the pocket edges, eliminating the eyelet. You may also serge-finish the outer caddy edge (step 8) instead of applying the eyelet. Use decorative thread in both loopers and serge-finish with wrong sides together using a wide, short, balanced 3-thread stitch. You'll need two spools of matching decorative thread, such as crochet thread, pearl cotton, or rayon.

2. Place the right side of Pocket One against the right side of the quilted rectangle with the cut edges 5-1/4" from the upper edge. Sew the pocket to the rectangle using a 1/4" seam allowance. (Fig. 2-28)

3. Press the pocket up. Top-stitch three vertical rows from the seamline to the folded pocket edge, creating four equal-sized pockets. Machine baste the outer pocket edges to the sides of the quilted rectangle, a little less than 1/4" from the cut edges.

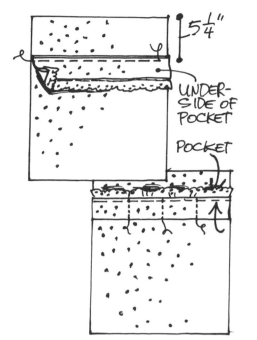

Fig. 2-28 Top-stitch the cut edges of the top pocket (Pocket One) to the quilted rectangle before pressing it up and stitching the vertical rows.

4. Place the cut edges of Pocket Two 2-3/4" below the bottom of the first pocket. Sew it in place using a 1/4" seam allowance. Press the pocket up and straight-stitch it into three 6"-wide pockets. Machine baste the outer edges to the side seam allowances.

5. Place the cut edges of Pocket Three 10-3/4" below the bottom of Pocket Two. Sew it in place as in step 4 but straight-stitch it into two equal-sized pockets.

6. Top-stitch the rougher hook side of the *Velcro* strip to the caddy, covering only the lower edge of Pocket Three. (Top-stitch sections of the loop side to any garment you want to hang from the caddy that doesn't already have a *Velcro* closure.) (Fig. 2-29)

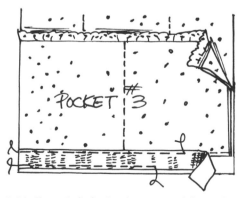

Fig. 2-29 Top-stitch the hook portion of the *Velcro* strip, just covering the lower edge of Pocket Three.

7. Round all four corners of both the quilted organizer and the other large rectangle of coordinating fabric.

8. Apply the wider eyelet around the outside of the caddy, beginning at the lower edge. Fold one end of the eyelet strip about 3/4" to the wrong side, place it on the organizer right sides together, and match the cut edges as you machine-baste it around the caddy. Overlap the remaining end 3/4" (without folding it back) as you complete the eyelet application.

9. Fold the three smaller rectangles in half crosswise with right sides together. Sew or serge both long sides. Turn each one right side out to form the straps.

10. Matching the cut edges, pin the straps to the wrong-side top edge of the caddy. Position a strap 2-1/2" from each side and center the remaining one between the other two.

11. Place the caddy and the other large (backing) rectangle right sides together with the eyelet sandwiched between. Sew or serge around all four sides, leaving an opening at the lower edge for turning. Turn the caddy right side out and hand-sew the opening closed.

12. Fold the hanger strips in half toward the back of the caddy. Apply snaps or buttons and buttonholes about 1/2" from the ends. (Fig. 2-30)

Fig. 2-30 Use snaps or buttons just above the caddy edge to secure the ends of the hanging straps.

Decorative Options

♦ Machine embroider or appliqué the baby's name on the lower pocket or pockets.

♦ Use a delicate decorative stitch instead of a straight-stitch when top-stitching.

♦ Decoratively serge-finish the upper pocket edges and the outer edge instead of applying the eyelet.

TOTE-ALONG SLEEPING BAG

Whip up a sleeping bag that rolls easily into a backpack for any youngster aged 2 to 6. An outside pocket stores any small sleep-over items (roll up more bulky pajamas or clothes inside the bag itself). Quilt a bright children's print to a soft flannel backing—it's fun, snuggly, and washes beautifully. (Fig. 2-31)

Fig. 2-31 Any youngster will be delighted with this surprisingly simple backpack sleeping bag.

Materials Needed

♦ 1-1/3 yards of bright-colored 45"-wide cotton/polyester fabric for the cover

♦ 1/3 yard of matching or coordinating print fabric for the outside pocket

♦ 1-1/3 yards of 45"-wide cotton flannel for the lining

♦ One crib-size or 45" by 60" sheet of polyester quilt batting

♦ 9" of 3/4"-wide *Velcro*

♦ 40" of 1"-wide cotton or polyester webbing

♦ One package of wide double-fold bias tape in a contrasting color

♦ One package of double-fold cotton quilt binding

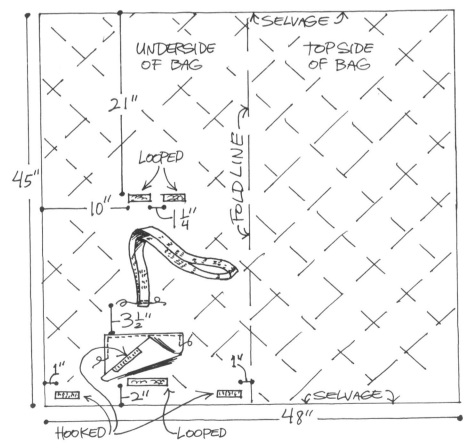

Fig. 2-32 Quilt the bag layers and transfer the placement markings.

Cutting Directions

♦ If not done previously, cut both the cover fabric and the flannel to 1-1/3 yard lengths.

♦ Cut one 14" by 10" rectangle for the pocket.

How-Tos

Sew or serge all seams using 1/4" allowances.

1. With the batting sandwiched between the wrong sides of the cover and lining, quilt through all layers. Use crossed diagonal rows of straight-stitching as far apart as 8", any other quilting design, or echo quilt around designs in the print. Then transfer the illustrated markings to the cover side of the quilt. (Fig. 2-32)

2. With right sides together, fold the pocket rectangle in half crosswise to make a rectangle 7" by 10". Seam the three sides, leaving an opening on the long edge for turning. Turn right side out and press.

3. Cut the *Velcro* into one 4" and two 2-1/2" pieces. Center the hooked side of the 4" piece on the wrong side of the long folded edge of the pocket. Top-stitch it in place.

4. Stitch the 2-1/2" *Velcro* hook pieces at both the lower-edge corners that will be the finished bag's underside, 1" from each side. (See Fig. 2-32) Stitch the 2-1/2" loop pieces 1-1/4" apart 21" from the upper edge and 10" from the side, as shown. Center and stitch the remaining 4" *Velcro* loop strip 2" above the lower edge.

5. Center the pocket over the 4" *Velcro* and top-stitch it in place.

6. Sew the webbing into a circle by lapping the ends 1/2" and zigzagging them together. Fold the circle in half with the seam on one end. Mark the opposite end. Top-stitch the marked fold 3-1/2" below the lower edge of the pocket.

7. Fold the bag in half the long way, flannel side out, and round the four outside corners. Beginning 18" from the top of the bag, bind the lower cut edges with the quilt binding, folding 3/4" to the wrong side at each end before stitching. (Fig. 2-33)

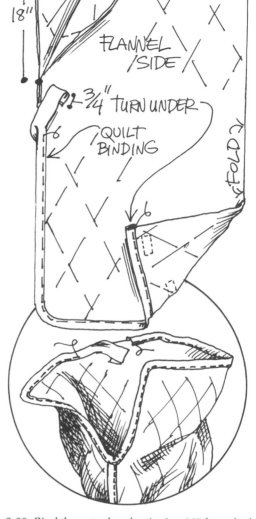

Fig. 2-33 Bind the cut edges beginning 18" from the bag top.

8. On one end of the double-fold bias binding, fold 3/4" to the wrong side. Starting at the fold of the bag, bind half of the upper edge, going down one side to the top of the quilt binding and back up again. Bind the remainder of the bag top, lapping the binding 3/4" at the end. Turn the bag right side out.

9. Center the webbing seam above the pocket at the lower edge. Straight-stitch through the strap and all layers of the bag underside to secure. (Fig. 2-34)

10. Make two lengthwise folds so the bag sides meet at the center, with the pockets and *Velcro* on the outside. Beginning at the upper edge, roll up the bag and secure it with the *Velcro*.

11. Pull the carrying straps around the bag so the pocket is right side up on the outside.

Decorative Options

♦ Echo quilt the body of the bag around the print background instead of using crossed diagonal lines of straight-stitching.

♦ Use a solid color for the bag cover and appliqué a name or a design to personalize the bag.

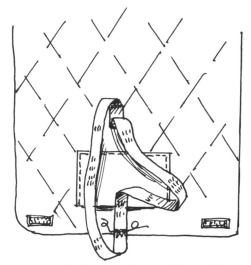

Fig. 2-34 Top-stitch the seamed area of the webbing straps through all layers at the bottom of the bag.

CHAPTER THREE
Gifts for Weddings and Brides

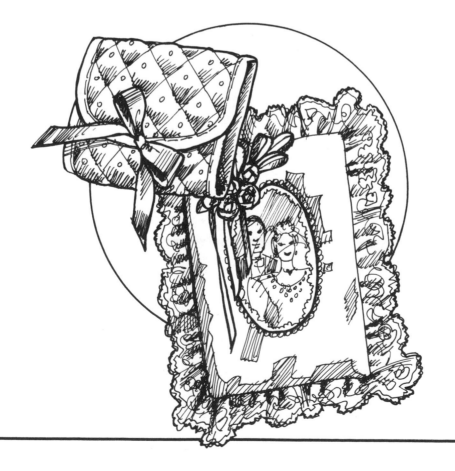

RING BEARER'S PILLOW

Apply a purchased floral appliqué as the centerpiece of this simply charming ring pillow or become a designer and add your own touches of machine embroidery or monogramming. The ribbons holding the rings become part of the design. (Fig. 3-1)

Fig. 3-1 Whether you use a simple appliqué or a more elaborate design, your handiwork will be a treasured part of the wedding.

Materials Needed

♦ 1/4 yard of 45"-wide fabric, such as satin or taffeta

♦ One yard of 1-1/2"- to 2"-wide ruffled lace with one scalloped edge

♦ 2-2/3 yards of 1/8"-wide satin ribbon

♦ One floral appliqué (or a grouping of appliqués) to fit the top of a 7-1/2"-square pillow

♦ Fiberfill for pillow stuffing

♦ Glue gun and glue

Cutting Directions

Cut two 8" squares from the fabric. Slightly round the corners.

How-Tos

Sew or serge using 1/4" seam allowances.

1. For the speediest application, glue the floral appliqué to the right side of one fabric square, keeping the design 1/2" from the cut edges to allow for ease in seaming and turning. You may choose to leave the outer appliqué edges loose for a three-dimensional effect. (If you prefer, top-stitch the appliqué to the pillow instead of gluing.)

2. Cut two 12" pieces of the ribbon to hold the rings, with the ends at an angle to prevent fraying. Fold each in half crosswise and top-stitch them across the folds at an

appropriate position on the appliqué. (Fig. 3-2)

AT LEAST 1/2"

Fig. 3-2 Top-stitch the center of the ribbons onto the pillow top to hold the rings.

3. Fold one end of the ruffled lace 1" to the wrong side. With right sides together and beginning at the center of one side, machine-baste the lace to the pillow top, easing around the corners and lapping the ends 1".

> **Serger tip:** Instead of using purchased ruffled lace, construct your own ruffle to match the pillow fabric by finishing one long edge of a 2-yard-long and 1-1/2"- to 2"-wide bias strip with a rolled edge and serge-gathering the opposite edge to fit the pillow top.

4. With right sides together, seam the pillow front to the pillow back, sewing or serging over the original basting line, making sure not to catch the ribbons or the lace in the seaming and leaving an opening for turning and stuffing.

5. Turn the pillow right side out and stuff it lightly. Hand-sew the opening closed.

6. Cut the remaining ribbon into four 18" pieces. Tie each piece into a bow and hand-sew one bow at each corner. Knot all of the ribbons 1/2" from the ends.

Decorative Options

♦ Design and construct a special appliqué instead of purchasing one.

♦ Use machine embroidery as part of the design. Add the couple's marriage date and their names or initials.

♦ Add pearls, beads, rosettes, or other decorative detail to your creation.

LACE-TRIMMED GARTER

It's a long-standing tradition—the bride must wear a garter. They are usually of frothy white lace and decorated for this special occasion. Make one in a jiffy using lace and ribbon. Decorate it with our simple bow and appliqué or add a more elaborate embellishment. (Fig. 3-3)

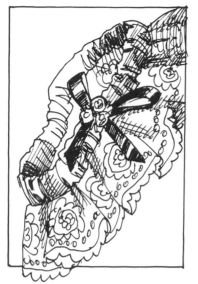

Fig. 3-3 Ribbon and lace are all it takes to make a pretty garter.

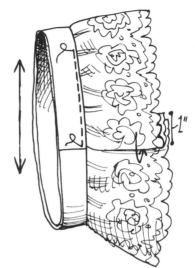

Fig. 3-4 Hold the ribbon circles taut as you top-stitch the lace between them.

Materials Needed

♦ 1-1/4 yards of 5/8"-wide satin ribbon

♦ 2/3 yard of 2"-wide ruffled lace with one scalloped edge

♦ 12" of 3/8"-wide elastic

♦ 9" of 1/4"-wide satin ribbon

♦ One small flower appliqué

How-Tos

1. Cut the 5/8"-wide ribbon into two 22" pieces. Using a 1/4" seam allowance, sew the ends of each piece together to form two circles.

2. Place the ribbon circles wrong sides together with the seams matching. Fold one end of the lace 1" to the wrong side and sandwich the straight edge between the ribbon layers. Top-stitch through the three layers, holding the ribbons taut and overlapping the ends of the lace 1". (Fig. 3-4)

3. Top-stitch the other long edges of the ribbon circles, leaving an opening for inserting the elastic.

> **Serger tip:** Decoratively serge-finish the ribbon circles together along the upper garter edge using a wide balanced stitch instead of top-stitching. You'll need two spools of matching or coordinating decorative thread, such as a shiny rayon.

4. Thread the elastic through the garter and sew the ends together to form a circle. Top-stitch the opening closed.

5. Tie the narrower ribbon into a bow. Glue or hand-sew it to the garter front with the flower appliqué over the center.

Decorative Options

♦ Glue or hand-sew more bows and flower appliqués at regular intervals all around the garter.

♦ Make a more elaborate bow using 3/4 yard each of pearl beading, 1/8"-wide satin ribbon, and 1/16"-wide satin ribbon. Glue or hand-sew them to the garter with a ribbon rosette in the center. (Fig. 3-5)

Fig. 3-5 Add more elaborate embellishment if desired.

FOND MEMORIES VIDEO BOX

Create a gift to delight the newlyweds and their friends and relatives as well—a video tape of the festivities enclosed in a beautifully decorated box. (Fig. 3-6)

Fig. 3-6 Add a simple appliqué to the covered video box or embellish it to your heart's desire.

Materials Needed

One vinyl video box

♦ 1/4 yard of satin fabric

1/4 yard of lace yardage

1/4 yard of batting

1-1/4 yards of 1"- to 2"-wide ruffled lace with one scalloped edge

1/2 yard of 1"-wide satin ribbon

Fusible transfer web for the appliqué

♦ Machine embroidery thread

Glue stick for glue-basting

♦ Glue gun and glue for permanent gluing

Cutting Directions

Cut the batting equal to the height and wrap-around width of the video box. (Fig. 3-7)

♦ Cut the fabric and lace 1" larger in both directions.

♦ Cut two 2-1/2" hearts from the remaining satin fabric following the pattern grid. (Fig. 3-7)

How-Tos

1. With the wrong side of the lace rectangle against the right side of the satin, machine-baste around the outer edges using a 1/4" seam allowance. Trim the allowance next to the basting line.

> **Serger tip:** To eliminate the trimming step, serge-finish the two rectangles together using a narrow balanced stitch and trimming the edges slightly.

2. Overlap the hearts and appliqué them to the lace side of the joined rectangles, positioning them so they will be centered on the top cover of the box. Machine-embroider the bride's name on one heart and the groom's name on the other.

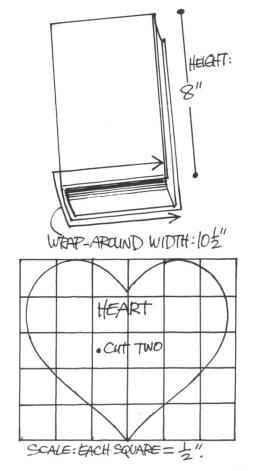

Fig. 3-7 Cut the batting the exact measurements of the box height and wrap around width. Cut the fabric 1" larger in both directions.

3. Glue-baste the batting to the outside of the box.

4. With the lace on the outside, glue the lace and satin rectangle over the batting, stretching it around the cover edge and securing it on the underside of the box lip.

5. Fold under 1/2" on one end of the lace. Beginning with the folded end at the bottom of the box, glue the lace straight edge over the edge of the lace and satin cover with the right side of the lace to the outside. Overlap the ends to finish. (Fig. 3-8)

6. Glue the satin ribbon around the uncovered portion of the box, turning both ends under 1/2".

Decorative Options

♦ Use your imagination and machine embroidery skills to create a more elaborate appliqué on the outside of the video box.

♦ Add pearls, purchased floral appliqués, or hand-embroidery to design an original keepsake.

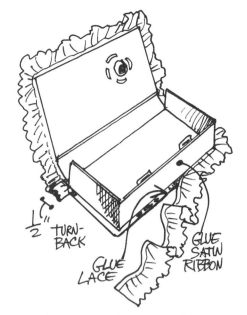

Fig. 3-8 Glue the lace edge over the fabric edge on the underside of the box lip, beginning and ending at the lower corner.

FLOWER GIRL'S BASKET

This ornate skirted basket is a thoughtful keepsake gift. Make the small size given here for the flower girl to carry or enlarge the dimensions for a basket to hold rice bundles or other wedding favors. (Fig. 3-9)

Fig. 3-9 Sewing and gluing are combined to decorate the basket quickly and easily.

Materials Needed

♦ One basket with symmetrical sides—approximately 4" deep and 6" in diameter at the top

♦ One 12" square of fleece

♦ 1/2 yard of 45"-wide fabric, such as taffeta

♦ 1-1/4 yards of 1"-wide flat lace with one scalloped edge

♦ 2/3 yard of 3/4"-wide ruffled lace

♦ 1-1/2 yards of 5/8"-wide satin ribbon

♦ 1-1/3 yards of 1/8"-wide satin ribbon

♦ 2/3 yard of 1"-wide satin ribbon

♦ 2/3 yard of 3/8"-wide clear elastic

♦ One 8" by 36" rectangle of tulle

♦ Two purchased wire-stemmed floral sprays

♦ Glue gun and glue

Cutting Directions

♦ Cut one fleece circle and one fabric circle with diameters equal to twice the depth of the basket plus the bottom measurement.

♦ Cut one fabric circle the same measurement plus 2" for the basket liner.

♦ Cut one fabric rectangle for the ruffle twice the circumference of the basket plus 1/2" by the depth of the basket minus 1/4".

♦ Cut the flat lace the same length as the ruffle. (Fig. 3-10)

Fig. 3-10 Measure the basket accurately before cutting out the ruffle, fleece, and fabric cover and liner.

How-Tos

1. Glue the fleece circle to the inside of the basket and the smaller fabric circle to the outside of the basket, easing the fabric evenly.

2. Around the larger fabric circle machine-baste gathering stitches 1" from the cut edge. Center the circle on the inside of the basket, pulling up the gathers to fit around the upper edge of the basket. Glue the liner in place on the inside rim. Fold the remainder of the circle to the outside of the basket (slitting the fabric for the handles) and glue it in place.

3. With right sides together, seam the flat lace to one long edge of the ruffle strip using a narrow seam allowance. Press the allowance toward the fabric and top-stitch close to the fold from the right side. (Fig. 3-11)

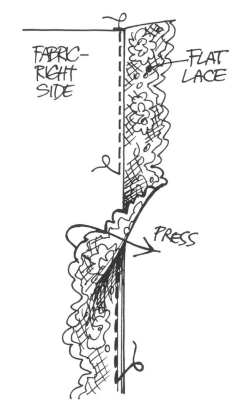

Fig. 3-11 Finish the ruffle strip by seaming the lace to one long edge, turning the allowance up, and top-stitching through it.

Serger tip: Substitute narrow balanced 3-thread seaming for the narrow conventional seaming in this project—no need to finish the allowances in the following step.

4. Seam the ruffle into a circle using a narrow seam and finish the seam allowances. Press 1/2" of the raw edge to the wrong side and quartermark it.

5. Quartermark the clear elastic and, matching their quartermarks, zigzag the elastic to the inside of the ruffle using a long medium-width stitch, stretching the elastic to fit the fabric. (Fig. 3-12)

6. Glue the elastic side of the ruffle to the upper basket edge. Glue the ruffled lace, right side out, over the upper edge of the ruffle, beginning and ending at one handle and overlapping the lace ends.

7. Wrap and glue the 5/8"-wide satin ribbon around the handle. Glue the ends to secure.

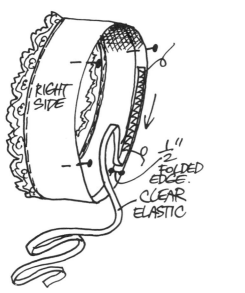

Fig. 3-12 Seam the elastic to the folded allowance at the top of the ruffle, matching quartermarks and stretching the elastic to fit.

8. Cut the tulle into two 18" pieces. Tie one piece loosely around the base of each handle. Twist a floral spray around the handles over each tulle knot. Cut the 1/8" ribbon into two equal lengths and tie a bow around the base of each handle.

9. Tie the 1"-wide ribbon into a bow at the top of the handle.

Decorative Options

♦ Tie long ribbon streamers to the basket handles before attaching the flowers and bows in step 8.

♦ Purchase additional floral sprays or a floral garland and decorate the entire basket handle.

VICTORIAN LINEN PRESS

For more than a century, smart housekeepers have been storing linens fresh and wrinkle-free by rolling them in a linen press. Any bride will treasure this practical gift—include some napkins and placemats, too. (Fig. 3-13)

Fig. 3-13 Press cherished linens between sheets of acid-free tissue for a truly novel gift.

Materials Needed

♦ One 18" mailing tube—at least 2" in diameter (found in office supply stores)

♦ 2/3 yard of 45"-wide or wider fabric, such as chintz or a cotton print

♦ 3/4 yard of 39"-wide or wider unbleached muslin or a coordinating 100% cotton print

♦ 2/3 yard of 1/2"-wide satin ribbon

♦ Glue stick

♦ Acid-free tissue paper

Cutting Directions

♦ Cut a 19" by 36" rectangle from both the muslin and the chintz.

♦ Cut two chintz circles 1" larger than the diameter of the tube.

♦ Cut one muslin rectangle 19" wide by twice the tube diameter plus 1" for the tube cover. (Fig. 3-14)

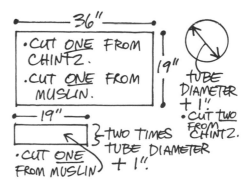

Fig. 3-14 Cut out the linen press pieces from muslin and a print fabric.

How-Tos

Sew or serge the seams using 1/2" allowances.

1. Center the wrong side of a fabric circle over each end of the tube. Stretch tightly around the ends and glue-baste the edges.

2. Press the smaller muslin rectangle in half lengthwise and then press 1/2" to the wrong side of each short end. (Fig. 3-15)

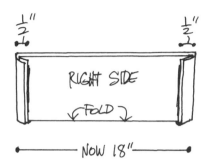

Fig. 3-15 Before covering the tube, prepare the smaller muslin rectangle.

3. Glue-baste the long cut edges to the tube, matching the short-end folds to the tube ends. Wrapping tightly, glue-baste the short ends to the tube.

4. Hand blind-stitch the long folded edge tightly over the cut edges, then blind-stitch around the tube ends. (Fig. 3-16)

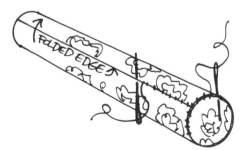

Fig. 3-16 Stretching firmly, blind-stitch the fabric tightly around the tube. Then blind-stitch the muslin to the fabric covering the ends.

5. Seam together the remaining chintz and muslin rectangles with right sides together, leaving an opening for turning. Trim the corners.

Serger tip: To eliminate the turning when seaming the rectangles, place them wrong sides together and decoratively serge-finish all edges together using a wide, satin-length, balanced 3-thread stitch. You'll need two spools of complementary decorative thread.

6. Turn the joined rectangles right side out and press carefully. Hand-sew the opening closed.

7. On the right side of the chintz, top-stitch the center of the ribbon to the center of one end. (Fig. 3-17)

Fig. 3-17 Top-stitch the ribbon tie to one end of the joined rectangles to hold them in place after wrapping the tube.

8. Layer the linens between sheets of acid-free tissue paper on the muslin side of the rectangle. Wrap them around the covered tube and tie them in place with the ribbon.

Decorative Options

♦ Use a solid-color polyester/cotton or linen in place of the chintz or cotton print. Add decorative machine stitching to embellish the press cover before beginning step 5.

♦ Using machine embroidery or built-in sewing machine lettering, monogram the outer layer of the cover.

SPECIAL KEEPSAKE BOX

She'll want to keep treasured mementos of the most important days of her romance in this pretty handmade box. It is softly padded and measures 4" by 4" by 3". Simply enlarge the measurements given to make a bigger box for storing love letters or larger photos. (Fig. 3-18)

Fig. 3-18 Give a gift she'll love forever—a padded box specially made to store all of her romantic keepsakes.

Materials Needed

♦ 1/3 yard of outer fabric, such as chintz or taffeta

♦ 1/3 yard of lining, such as muslin or satin

♦ 1/3 yard of polyester batting

♦ One 10" by 13" sheet of plastic canvas

♦ 2 yards of satin or cotton cording

♦ 2-1/2" of 1/8"-wide white elastic

♦ One 1/2" ball button

♦ One 4" lace doily

♦ Glue gun and glue

Cutting Directions

♦ Cut one box from the outer fabric, one box from the lining, and two boxes from the batting using the pattern grid. (Fig. 3-19)

♦ Cut four 2-5/8" by 4-3/8" rectangles and three 4-1/2" squares from the plastic canvas. Trim the pieces so all edges are smooth.

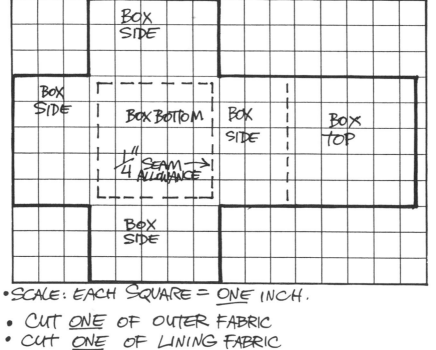

- SCALE: EACH SQUARE = ONE INCH.
- CUT ONE OF OUTER FABRIC
- CUT ONE OF LINING FABRIC
- CUT TWO OF BATTING

Fig. 3-19 Cut out the box layers following the pattern grid.

How-Tos

Sew or serge the seams using 1/4" allowances.

1. Sandwich the outer fabric and liner right sides together between the two batting pieces. Seam, leaving a 4" opening on one long edge for turning and inserting the plastic canvas.

2. Clip the inside corners and trim the outside corners. Turn the fabric right side out.

3. Insert a small plastic canvas piece into the front and sides of the box, between the batting layers. After inserting, stitch from the right side across the bottom edges of the box next to the canvas. (Fig. 3-20)

4. Insert two plastic squares into the box bottom.

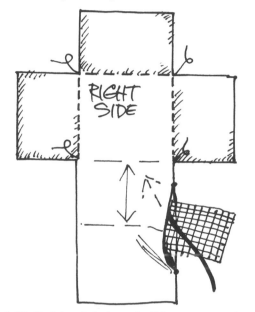

Fig. 3-20 Straight-stitch through all layers next to the canvas after inserting it into the sides and front.

Stitch across the remaining bottom edge to enclose the squares. Repeat for the box top and back. Hand-sew the opening closed.

5. Hand-sew the four vertical edges of the box together. Glue the cording to all edges of the box and around the top.

6. Form the 1/8"-wide elastic into a loop and glue or

hand-sew it to the underside of the box top. Sew the button to a corresponding position on the box front. Hand-sew the lace doily onto the box top. (Fig. 3-21)

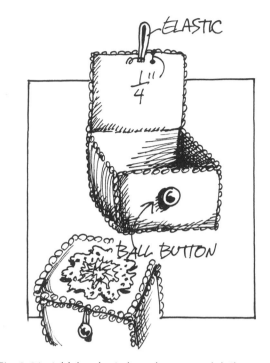

Fig. 3-21 Add the elastic loop, button, and doily to complete the project.

Decorative Options

♦ Substitute pearl beading for the cording when decorating the box edges.

♦ Create an elaborate appliqué for the box top in place of the doily.

HANDY HOSIERY ORGANIZER

This pocketed organizer is a welcome shower gift for the bride who is headed on a honeymoon. The six vinyl pockets will keep her hosiery so organized that she will want to continue using it when she returns home. (Fig. 3-22)

Fig. 3-22 Combine quilted cotton and vinyl for a gift that keeps delicate hosiery snag-free.

Materials Needed

♦ 1/4 yard of 45"-wide double-faced quilted cotton fabric

♦ 1/3 yard of 54"-wide lightweight clear or white vinyl (use a vinyl mattress cover if yardage is unavailable)

♦ 3-1/4 yards of 5/8"-wide satin ribbon

Cutting Directions

♦ Cut one 8" by 17-1/2" rectangle from the quilted fabric.

♦ Cut two 6-1/2" by 12" rectangles, one 6-1/2" by 6" rectangle, and two 6-1/2" by 11" rectangles from the vinyl.

How-Tos

When sewing on the vinyl, use a sharp needle and a long (8 stitches per inch) stitch length.

1. Fold and press the ribbon lengthwise slightly less than halfway across. (Fig. 3-23)

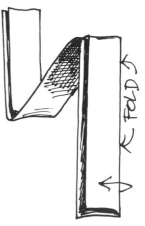

Fig. 3-23 When folding the ribbon lengthwise, extend one edge slightly past the other.

2. Place the folded ribbon over the short ends of the 6-1/2" by 12" vinyl rectangles with the narrowest width of the ribbon on top. Top-stitch to bind the edges. Repeat for one 6-1/2" side of the smallest rectangle.

> **Serger tip:** Eliminate the ribbon and decoratively serge-bind all the edges using a wide, satin-length, balanced 3-thread stitch. You'll need two spools of heavier decorative thread, such as pearl cotton or pearl rayon.

3. On the two 6-1/2" by 11" vinyl rectangles, draw lines the length of the rectangle 2-1/4" from the cut edges. (Fig. 3-24)

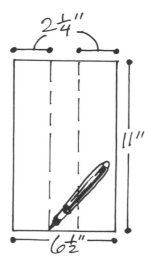

Fig. 3-24 Use a pen or marker to draw lines on the 6-1/2" by 11" vinyl rectangles.

4. Crease the vinyl on the marked lines. Center the long edge of one 6-1/2" by 12" vinyl rectangle on one of the creased lines, beginning and ending 1/2" from the bound edges. Beginning at the top, bind the creased edge as in steps 1 and 2, turning both ribbon ends 1/2" to the wrong side. (Fig. 3-25)

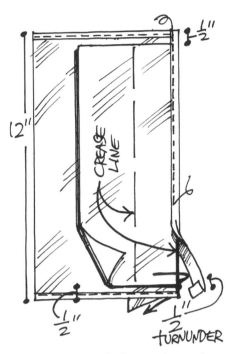

Fig. 3-25 Center one marked rectangle on a larger rectangle, wrapping the edge at one marked line. Using the ribbon, bind the edge through all layers.

5. Center one long edge of the other 6-1/2" by 12" vinyl rectangle on the other creased line. Bind the folded edge as in step 4.

6. Align the two long bound edges and fold out the long cut edge of the vinyl on the top side. Fold the edge in half crosswise and center the lower edge

corner of the smaller bound rectangle in the fold, matching and binding the outside cut edges as in the previous steps. (Fig. 3-26)

Fig. 3-26 Fold out the unattached section of vinyl on top of the bound layers. Then fold it in half and bind the smaller rectangle between the outer edges.

7. Repeat steps 4 through 6 on the other side of the organizer.

8. Fold out the remaining long cut edges of the 6-1/2" by 11" vinyl rectangles. Match and pin the vinyl edges to the long edges of the quilted rectangle, beginning 3/4" from one short end of the quilted rectangle. (Place the pins inside the 1/4" seam allowances.)

9. Gently round all four corners of the quilted rectangle. Beginning in the center of one long edge, continuously bind the entire outer edge, catching the vinyl and easing the binding around the corners. Turn the end of the binding under 1/2" and lap it over the beginning of the binding for 1/2".

10. Cut the remaining ribbon into two equal pieces. On the right side center of the flap, mark 1" from the bound edge for the ribbon placement. Mark the second ribbon placement 1-1/2" up from the folded bottom edge. Top-stitch both ribbons to the organizer in the marked positions, folding under 1/2" on each. (Fig. 3-27)

Decorative Options

♦ Prior to step 8, add a monogram to the quilted rectangle, positioning it to fall in the area above the tie on the organizer flap.

♦ Make a unique quilted fabric by sandwiching batting between chintz or a cotton print and a backing fabric such as fusible interfacing. Echo quilt around the pattern from the right side.

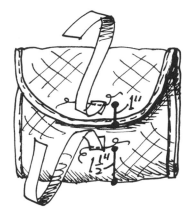

Fig. 3-27 Top-stitch the ribbon tie ends to the quilted cover.

WEDDING-PICTURE FRAME

Give the bride and groom a special place to display their favorite 5" by 7" wedding photo. This fanciful padded frame adds a romantic touch. Much simpler than it appears, the project requires little sewing but lots of speedy gluing. (Fig. 3-28)

Fig. 3-28 Fond memories look even sweeter in a lavish wedding-picture frame.

Materials Needed

♦ 1/3 yard of fabric, such as taffeta or satin

♦ 2/3 yard of 1/2"-wide ruffled lace

♦ 1-1/3 yards of 2"-wide ruffled lace with one scalloped edge

♦ One yard of 5/8"-wide satin ribbon

♦ One yard of 1/8"-wide satin ribbon

♦ 2/3 yard of pearl beading

♦ One 8" by 10" rectangle of polyester batting

♦ One 8" by 10" sheet of clear acetate (purchased from office supply sources)

♦ Two 8" by 10" rectangles and one 4" by 7" rectangle of heavyweight cardboard or matte board (A purchased matte board with an oval opening may be used instead of one 8" by 10" rectangle.)

♦ Glue stick for glue-basting

♦ Glue gun and glue for gluing

♦ Water-soluble marker

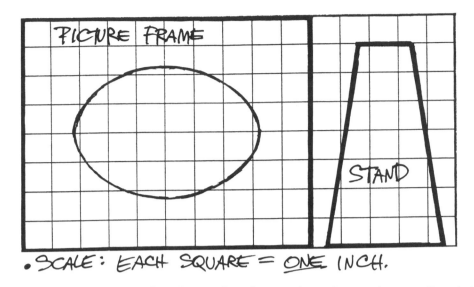

Fig. 3-29 Cut the stand from the smaller cardboard rectangle and cut out the oval on one larger cardboard piece to make the frame front.

Cutting Directions

♦ For the frame front, cut an oval from one of the 8" by 10" cardboard rectangles following the pattern grid. (Fig. 3-29)

♦ Cut the stand from the smaller cardboard rectangle. (Fig. 3-29)

♦ Cut two 10" by 12" fabric rectangles and two fabric pieces 1/2" larger than the stand on all sides.

How-Tos

1. Place the frame front right side down on the batting rectangle, matching the cut edges. Trace the oval opening using the marker and trim away the batting inside the opening.

2. Center the frame front on the wrong side of one 10" by 12" fabric rectangle. Using the marker, trace the oval opening on the fabric and add a 1" allowance inside the oval to draw the cutting line. (Fig. 3-30)

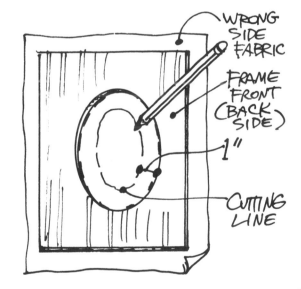

Fig. 3-30 Mark the oval opening and a cutting line 1" inside the oval opening.

3. Trim away the fabric on the cutting line and clip the allowance to within 1/8" of the oval opening. (Fig. 3-31)

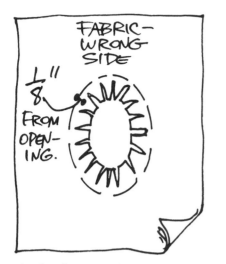

Fig. 3-31 Clip the allowance after trimming the fabric away on the cutting line.

4. Using the glue stick, glue-baste the batting to the frame front.

5. Place the batting side of the front on the wrong side of the trimmed fabric, matching the oval openings. Fold the clipped allowance to the wrong side of the frame front and glue it in place with the glue gun. Repeat for the outer edges, stretching the fabric evenly when gluing.

6. Glue the narrow lace to the opening by folding 1/2" of one end to the underside, gluing the right side of the lace to the wrong side of the oval opening

(with the ruffle inside the opening), and lapping the ends 1/2". (Fig. 3-32)

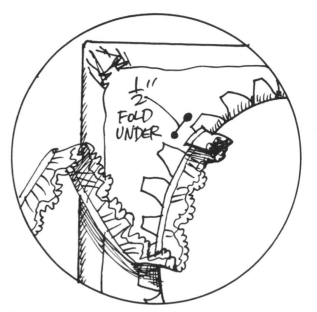

Fig. 3-32 Glue the narrow lace edge over the clipped allowance on the underside of the frame front.

7. On the right side, glue the pearl beading to the edge of the oval opening.

8. Fold one end of the wider lace 1" to the wrong side and, beginning at the lower edge of the frame front, glue the straight edge of the right side of the lace to the underside of the frame, easing the lace at the corners and overlapping the ends 1".

9. Attach the acrylic sheet to the back of the frame by gluing it only at the corners.

10. Center the remaining cardboard rectangle over the wrong side of the second fabric rectangle. Glue the edges in place on the underside, stretching evenly.

11. Glue one fabric stand cover to the stand. On the other fabric stand cover, press 1/2" to the wrong side on all edges and, with wrong sides together, glue it to the uncovered side of the stand.

12. To make a hinge for the stand, cut one 1-1/2" and one 4-1/2" piece from the 5/8"-wide ribbon. Center the stand on the frame back, matching the lower edges. Fold the 1-1/2" piece of ribbon in half. With the fold toward the top of the frame, glue half of the ribbon to the upper edge of the stand and the other half to the frame back. (Fig. 3-33)

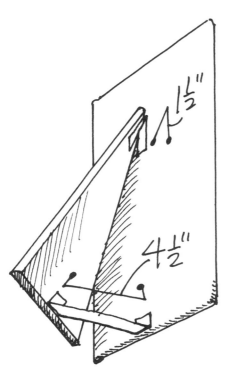

Fig. 3-33 Use ribbon and glue to hinge the stand to the frame.

13. To complete the stand, glue the 4-1/2" ribbon piece to the center of the lower edges of the frame and stand.

14. Glue the edges of the frame back to the frame front, leaving the upper edge open for inserting the picture.

15. Cut the remaining 5/8"-wide ribbon into three 10" pieces. Sew each into a circle using a 1/8" seam allowance.

16. Machine-baste next to the inner edge of each ribbon circle. Pull the threads to gather each one tightly into a rosette, knotting securely. (Fig. 3-34)

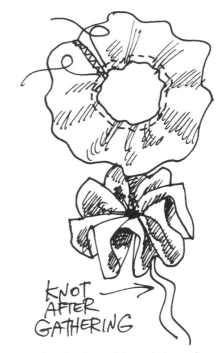

Fig. 3-34 Gather the three ribbon circles to form rosettes.

17. Fold the 1/8"-wide ribbon into a decorative bow with several loops at the top and tails 5" to 6" long. Glue the center of the bow to an upper corner of the oval opening. Glue the ribbon rosettes over the center of the bow.

Decorative Options

♦ Add a second narrower row of lace to the outer frame edge in step 8 to create a layered effect.

♦ Use pearl beading to enhance the bow in step 17 or glue an additional row around the outer frame edge next to the lace.

CHAPTER FOUR
Gifts with a Feminine Flair

FANCY HAIR BOW

Sew or serge a quick and easy gift just like the expensive versions found in accessories departments and specialty stores. You'll be delighted with the results. (Fig. 4-1)

Fig. 4-1 Use chiffon or any decorative fabric to make a pretty elasticized hair bow.

Materials Needed

♦ 1/3 yard of lightweight 45"-wide fabric, such as chiffon, metallic, or organza

♦ 7" of 1/4"-wide braided or clear elastic

Cutting Directions

♦ Cut one 8" by 33" fabric rectangle for the bow.

♦ Cut one 2-1/2" by 36" fabric strip for the elastic cover.

Note: For a heavier or stiffer fabric such as taffeta, cut the bow rectangle 8" by 30" and the strip 2-1/2" by 27".

How-Tos

1. Fold the narrower rectangle in half lengthwise with right sides together. Beginning and ending 1" from each end, seam the long edges using a 1/4" allowance.

2. Turn the tube right side out. Sew the short ends right sides together using a 3/8" seam allowance. (Fig. 4-2)

3. Thread the elastic through the opening of the tube and knot securely. Hand-sew or edge-stitch the opening closed.

4. Finish the larger rectangle by pressing 1/8" to the wrong side on each short end and edge-stitching. Press under another 1/8" and edge-stitch again, creating a double hem. Repeat for the two longer sides.

5. Thread the finished rectangle through the tube circle and tie it into a bow.

> **Serger tips:** Construct the tube and bow by serge-seaming and serge-finishing using a rolled edge. Adjust the serger for a medium- to short-length 3-thread rolled-edge stitch, using matching serger or lightweight thread. Test the serging on a fabric scrap to make sure it does not pull off the edge. If it does, lengthen and/or widen the stitch. To serge the hair bow:
>
> 1. With right sides together, serge-seam the short ends of the narrow strip to form a circle.
> 2. Knot the elastic into a circle and wrap the fabric strip wrong sides together over the elastic, matching the seamlines. Serge-seam the cut edges, lapping the ends of the stitching.
> 3. Serge-finish the two long edges of the larger rectangle. Repeat for the short ends. Dab seam sealant at the corners and allow it to dry before clipping the thread chains and tying the rectangle around the elastic tube.

Decorative Options

♦ Top-stitch the hems in step 4 using decorative machine stitching.

♦ Decoratively serge-finish the bow edges using metallic or heavy rayon thread in the upper looper or serge over lightweight flexible beading when finishing the ends. To apply beading most easily, use a beading foot (if available for your serger).

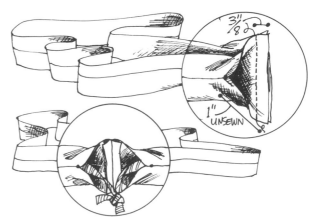

Fig. 4-2 Sew the tube ends together then thread and knot the elastic and hand-sew the opening closed.

WEIGHTED SCISSOR TENDER

A thoughtful gift for a seamstress of any experience level, this nifty weight keeps scissors or clippers right at her fingertips. Simple to make, you can whip up several out of scraps on hand. (Fig. 4-3)

Fig. 4-3 Make a tiny scissor tender that packs a lot of weight.

Materials Needed

♦ 1/4 yard (or a 7" scrap) of fabric

♦ One 7" piece of fusible tricot interfacing

♦ 2/3 yard of 1-1/2"- to 2"-wide ruffled lace with one scalloped edge

♦ 1 yard of 1/4"-wide matching or coordinating ribbon

♦ 2 yards of filler cord, such as crochet thread or pearl cotton

♦ Polyester fiberfill

♦ One large ball (or roller) bearing for weight

Cutting Directions

♦ Cut one 6-1/2" circle from the fabric and one from the interfacing.

♦ Cut the ribbon into one 6" and one 30" piece.

How-Tos

1. Fuse the interfacing to the wrong side of the fabric circle.

2. Fold one end of the lace 1/2" to the wrong side. With wrong sides together, seam the lace to the circle using a 1/8" seam allowance, easing the lace to the circle, and lapping the ends.

> **Serger tip:** Serge-seam the lace to the circle using a narrow, medium-length, balanced stitch.

3. Press the seam allowance toward the fabric and, from the wrong side, top-stitch the seam near the fold, catching the allowance. (Fig. 4-4)

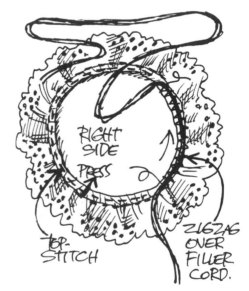

Fig. 4-4 Position the seam allowance and gathering cord on the right side—the ribbon will hide them.

4. From the right side, zigzag over two strands of filler cord placed on the seam allowance, being careful not to catch the cord in the stitching.

5. Pull up the filler cord slightly to form a bag for the ball bearing. Wrap the bearing in the fiberfill and insert it into the bag. Pull the cord to close the top of the bag and knot it securely. Clip the ends. **Note:** If you are unable to pull the bag completely closed, hand-sew to close it tightly.

6. Wrap the end of the longer ribbon piece around the gathering stitches and knot it securely, allowing the opposite end to hang freely. Hand-sew the knot to secure it.

7. Tie the shorter ribbon piece into a bow and hand-sew it over the first ribbon knot. Tie the free end of the long ribbon to a pair of scissors or clippers.

> **Serger tip:** Cut one 10" circle from fabric with no definite right or wrong side and one 6" circle from the fusible interfacing. Center and fuse the interfacing to the wrong side of the circle. Adjust the serger for a 3-thread rolled edge, using decorative thread in the upper looper. From the right side, serge-finish the edge. If available, adjust the differential feed to the

> lowest setting to prevent puckering. Serge slowly and pull the fabric straight in front of the presser foot to perfect the stitch. Use a water-soluble marker to draw a line on the right side of the fabric 2" from the rolled edge. Place the cording on the marking and zigzag as in step 4. Complete the project, following the instructions for sewing.

Decorative Options

♦ Use a beading strand, tulle, and a floral spray to further embellish the scissor tender.

♦ Serge a self-ruffle (instead of attaching scalloped lace) by cutting a larger circle and applying a rolled-edge finish as described after step 7.

COVERED ACCORDION FILE

Give her a special place to organize recipes, checks, coupons, or photos. The decorative cover adds a pretty handcrafted touch. She'll think of you every time she finds the contents right at her fingertips. (Fig. 4-5)

Fig. 4-5 Combine glamour and practicality in this embellished accordion file.

Materials Needed

♦ One accordion file—9" by 5-1/2"

♦ 3/8 yard of solid-color or striped fabric

♦ 1/4 yard of lightweight fusible interfacing

♦ 4 yards of satin cording

♦ Glue stick for glue-basting

♦ Rubber cement

Cutting Directions

♦ Fuse the interfacing to the wrong side of the fabric.

♦ Cut one rectangle two times the file-front height plus 2" by the file-front width plus 2".

♦ Cut two rectangles 1/2" larger than the file-front height and width.

How-Tos

1. On the large rectangle, press-mark vertical lines 1-1/4" to 1-1/2" apart (or use the stripes in the fabric as a guide). Glue-baste the satin cording on the marked lines. Allow the glue to dry, then zigzag top-stitch each row of cording to the fabric using a long wide stitch.

Serger tips: Make the cording (instead of purchasing it). Adjust for a short, narrow, 3-thread stitch with medium- to heavyweight rayon thread in the upper looper. Tighten the lower looper (as for a rolled edge) and serge over two strands of matching filler cord to create four yards.

Or, instead of applying cording, fold the fabric wrong sides together and flatlock on the marked lines using a 3-thread stitch and mediumweight rayon thread in the upper looper. Adjust for a short, medium- to narrow-width stitch. Allow the stitches to hang off the edge for the flattest flatlocking.

2. For the front and back covers, trim the two embellished rectangles to the file-front measurement plus 1" in both directions.

3. Use rubber cement to glue a cover to both the front and back of the file, wrapping 1/2" around each edge to the back side. Use clothespins to hold the edges in place until dry. (Fig. 4-6)

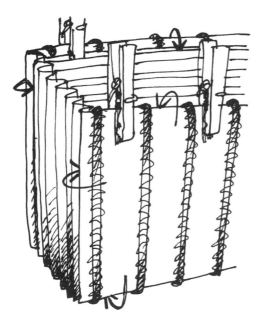

Fig. 4-6 After gluing the covers to the front and back, hold the edges in place with clothespins until dry.

4. On the two remaining rectangles, press all the edges 3/8" to the wrong side and edge-stitch to hem.

Serger tip: Serge-finish the edges of all four rectangles using a wide, medium-length, balanced 3- or 3/4-thread stitch and just skimming the edge with the knives. The serge-finishing will prevent raveling of the corded embellishment and will make it easier to turn the smaller rectangles for edge-stitching.

5. Spread rubber cement on the wrong side of the hemmed rectangles and glue them to the reverse side of the front and back covers, covering the upper raw edges of the covers.

6. Using a scissor tip, punch a hole in the center of the front and back covers 3/4" from the upper edge. Cut the remaining cording into two pieces approximately 12" long. Insert one end of each piece through a hole and knot it on the inside of the cover. Knot the other end to match and tie the two pieces into a bow. (Fig. 4-7)

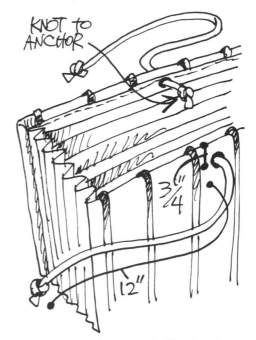

KNOT to ANCHOR

3/4"

12"

Fig. 4-7 Use satin cording to tie the file closed.

Decorative Options

♦ Instead of adding cording to the file cover, decorate the cover with machine embroidery, monogramming, or appliqué.

♦ Use your serger to decoratively flatlock the file cover or to make serger cording as described after step 1.

FLORAL-PRINT FAN

This French-inspired fan adds a delicate touch to any decor. Give it to a friend or relative who loves the feminine look—she can hang it on a wall or use it as a tabletop accent. (Fig. 4-8)

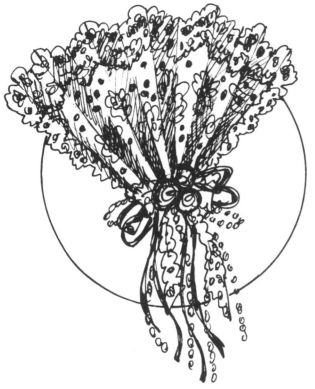

Fig. 4-8 Team lace, ribbons, pearl beading, and flowers with a floral-print fabric for a romantic fan.

Materials Needed

♦ 1/3 yard of decorative fabric, such as a floral print or moiré taffeta

♦ 1/3 yard of heavy fusible interfacing

♦ 1/3 yard of paper-backed fusible web

♦ 1/2 yard of 3"-wide flat lace with two scalloped edges

♦ 2-1/2 yards of 3/4"-wide flat lace with one scalloped edge

♦ 2 yards of 1/8"-wide satin ribbon

♦ 2 yards of pearl beading

♦ One silk floral spray in a coordinating color

♦ Pinking shears (optional)

Cutting Directions

Cut two 16" by 12" rectangles from the fabric, one from the interfacing, and one from the fusible web.

How-Tos

1. Fuse the interfacing to the wrong side of one fabric rectangle. Fuse the paper-backed web to the interfacing. Remove the paper and fuse the web to the wrong side of the other fabric rectangle.

2. Cut a 15" by 11" rectangle from the fused fabric. If available, use pinking shears to trim and neaten all four edges.

> **Serger tip:** Instead of pinking, serge-finish the edges using a medium-width, medium-length, balanced 3-thread stitch and matching thread.

3. Beginning at the upper right-hand corner, lap the wrong side of the narrower lace 1/4" over the short end of the fused fabric rectangle, with 1/2" extending past the fabric edge. Using a medium-width zigzag stitch, top-stitch the lace to the fabric. Repeat for the opposite end.

4. Trim around the pattern motif on the wider lace, shaping the ends to fit one long edge of the fabric rectangle (or turn 1/2" to the wrong side on each end). Lap the lace halfway over the top of the rectangle. Zigzag the lace along the top of the rectangle and again along the lower edge of the lace. (Fig. 4-9)

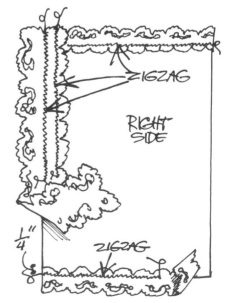

Fig. 4-9 Top-stitch the narrower lace to the sides before top-stitching the wider lace on top.

5. Fold and press the rectangle into 3/4" vertical pleats. Hand-sew the lower edges together. Tie the remaining lace around the lower edge, forming a bow. Cut both the narrow ribbon and the pearls into two equal sections and tie each into a bow over the lace bow. Hand-sew the silk flowers over the bow centers.

Decorative Options

♦ Use a solid-color fabric for the fan and use machine embroidery to decorate it after completing step 1.

♦ Make tiny sachets of potpourri and tie them onto the ends of the satin-ribbon bows for a sweet-scented fan.

QUIET-TIME PILLOW

She'll sleep late peacefully or just enjoy a little time to herself when she hangs this thoughtful gift on her doorknob. Simply add the "Please do not disturb" embroidery or embellish the pillow lavishly. (Fig. 4-10)

Fig. 4-10 Give a gift to relieve stress—it's a pretty decorative accent, too!

Materials Needed

♦ 1/6 yard of polyester/cotton, satin, or taffeta

♦ 3/4 yard of 1"- to 1-1/2"-wide flat lace with one scalloped edge

♦ 3 yards of 1/8"-wide satin ribbon

♦ Polyester fiberfill

Cutting Directions

♦ Cut two 6" by 4-1/2" fabric rectangles.

♦ Cut the ribbon into three 1-yard lengths.

How-Tos

1. To make the pillow top, embellish the right side of one rectangle by machine-embroidering "Please do not disturb" and adding decorative machine embroidery around the lettering.

2. Fold 1/2" of the lace to the wrong side. Right sides together, matching raw edges, and beginning at the center bottom of the pillow, machine-baste the lace to the pillow top using a 1/4" seam allowance, easing additional lace in at each corner, and lapping the lace ends. **Note:** To ease in the lace at each corner, sew to within 1/2" of the corner. Using a pin, ease in an extra 1/2" of lace while seaming to the corner. Pivot the fabric at the corner and again ease in an additional 1/2" while sewing the next 1/4" to 1/2". (Fig. 4-11)

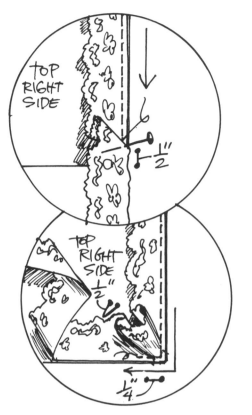

Fig. 4-11 Ease in an extra 1/2" of lace on both sides of the corners as you sew around them.

3. Matching the cut ends of the three ribbon lengths, place them 1-1/2" in from each corner over the lace at the top of the pillow to form a loop. Machine-baste them into position over the previous stitching. (Fig. 4-12)

4. With right sides together and matching cut edges, seam the pillow top to the other fabric rectangle, sewing over the basting stitches and being careful not to catch the lace or ribbons in the stitching. Leave an opening on the lower edge for turning.

Serger tip: Serge-seam instead of straight-stitching, using a medium-length, medium- to wide-width, balanced 3- or 3/4-thread stitch.

---

5. Turn the pillow right side out and stuff it with fiberfill. Hand-sew the opening closed. Cut the ribbon loops in half and tie the loose ends into a bow.

Decorative Options

♦ Instead of using machine embroidery for the "Please do not disturb" lettering, quickly top-stitch or hand-sew a lace or Battenberg motif to the pillow top, being careful not to place it within the seam allowances.

♦ Machine-embroider the "Please do not disturb" message between rows of decorative flatlocking on the pillow top. Mark diagonal lines 1-1/2" apart and flatlock over them (folded wrong sides together) before doing the lettering.

♦ If machine embroidery is not your forte, substitute fabric paint or hand embroidery for the lettering and design.

Fig. 4-12 Machine-baste the three ribbon ties to the pillow-front seamline.

LACE-TRIMMED CROISSANT COZY

Want a gift for the woman who enjoys elegant dining? Make this unusual bun warmer to hold six croissants at breakfast or even more biscuits and small rolls for tea or dinner. (Fig. 4-13)

Fig. 4-13 Make a case for croissants or other small pastries by sewing together three lacy circles and tying the center with ribbons.

Materials Needed

♦ One Battenberg lace or cutwork doily—11" to 14" in diameter

♦ 1/2 yard of woven cotton fabric

♦ 2-1/2 yards of 3/8"- to 1/2"-wide flat lace with one scalloped edge

♦ One yard of 1/4"-wide ribbon

Cutting Directions

♦ Cut two fabric circles 3/8" smaller in diameter than the doily.

♦ Cut the ribbon into six 6" pieces.

How-Tos

1. Fold one end of the lace to the wrong side. With right sides together, sew the lace to one fabric circle using a 1/8" seam allowance, easing the lace to the circle, and lapping the ends. Repeat for the other circle.

Serger tip: Serge-seam the lace to the fabric circle using a narrow-width, medium-length, balanced 3-thread stitch. Or place the lace and fabric wrong sides together and serge-seam, using a satin-length rolled edge for a more decorative finish.

2. Press the seam allowance to the wrong side of one circle and top-stitch through it close to the fold of the fabric. Repeat for the other circle.

3. Fold and press-mark one lace-trimmed circle in twelve equidistant sections and the doily into six equidistant sections.

4. With the doily and the unmarked circle right sides together, straight-stitch on each of the six lines marked on the doily to within 1-1/2" of the center. (Fig. 4-14)

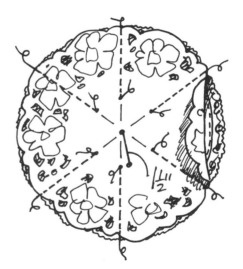

Fig. 4-14 Attach the outer doily layer to the unmarked fabric circle by top-stitching on the press-marks.

5. Position one of the ribbon pieces right sides together with one of the markings on the remaining fabric circle, matching the ribbon cut edge to the top-stitched folded edge. Seam the ribbon to the circle, using a 1/8" allowance. Fold the ribbon over the stitching and top-stitch next to the fold. Repeat at every second marking using the remaining ribbon pieces. (Fig. 4-15)

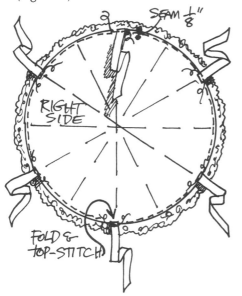

Fig. 4-15 Sew the ribbons to the press-marked fabric circle.

6. Layer the circle with the ribbons right side down over the other fabric circle (with the doily on the bottom). Match the ribbon placements to the sewn lines on the joined pieces. Sew through the two fabric circles only (not the doily) on the unstitched markings to within 2-1/4" of the center. (Fig. 4-16)

7. Press carefully to eliminate the marked lines. Tie the ribbons into three bows, joining the ends directly opposite each other to form the pockets.

Decorative Options

♦ If a doily is unavailable, cut three 11"- to 14"-diameter woven cotton circles and purchase an additional 1-1/4 yards of lace. (The fabric yardage is sufficient for three circles.) Embellish the third circle with decorative machine stitching to replace the doily.

♦ Decoratively serge-finish the edges of the woven cotton circles using a rolled edge instead of applying lace.

Serger tip: Cut the circles the same measurement as the lace doily. Adjust your serger for a satin-length 3-thread rolled edge with rayon thread in the upper looper. To perfect the stitch, you may need to use woolly or monofilament nylon thread in the lower looper. Serge slowly around the circle, pulling the fabric straight in front of the needle for the most even stitching.

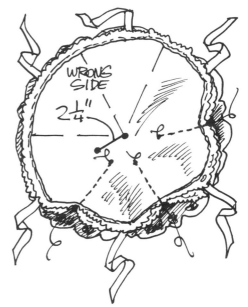

Fig. 4-16 Following the remaining press-marks on the top fabric circle, sew six short seams to join it to the middle circle.

DECORATOR DOORSTOP

Display your handiwork on the top of this striking doorstop. It functions as both a useful household item and an attractive decorative accent. (Fig. 4-17)

Fig. 4-17 Cover a brick with embellished fabric and coordinating braid for a weighty gift.

Materials Needed

♦ 1/6 yard of decorative fabric, such as moiré taffeta or satin

♦ 1/6 yard of fusible fleece (or 1/6 yard of polyester fleece and 1/3 yard of fusible web)

♦ One spool of matching or coordinating *Ribbon Floss* thread

♦ One piece of rubber gripper fabric 5" by 10" (or 1/6 yard) (available in fabric stores or by mail order)

♦ 3/4 yard of 1/2"-wide braid (upholstery braid works well)

♦ One brick or concrete block–approximately 8" by 4" by 3"

♦ Glue gun and glue

Cutting Directions

♦ Cut one fusible fleece rectangle for the doorstop bottom measuring the length and width of the brick.

♦ Cut one gripper fabric rectangle 3/4" larger than the length and width of the fleece rectangle.

♦ All other cutting will be done after fusing.

How-Tos

1. Fuse the fleece to the wrong side of the decorative fabric, following the manufacturer's instructions.

2. From the fused fabric, cut the first rectangle the circumference of the brick (around all four sides) plus 3/4" by the height of the brick plus 1". From the remaining fused fabric, cut a second rectangle for the brick top measuring 1" longer and wider than the brick.

3. On one short end of the first fused rectangle, fold and glue 3/4" to the wrong side. Glue the rectangle around the sides of the brick with 1/2" wrapped and glued to both the top and underside of the brick. Begin and end at one corner, lapping the folded end over the unfinished end and gluing securely.

4. Decoratively stitch the second rectangle for the brick top, giving it a quilted effect. Draw a stitching design on the fleece side of the fused rectangle. Thread *Ribbon Floss* on the bobbin and all-purpose thread in the needle. Test different types of decorative stitching on scraps of the fused fabric with the fabric side down, adjusting the stitch width and length. After achieving the desired look, embellish the rectangle, sewing over the design lines on the fleece side. (Fig. 4-18)

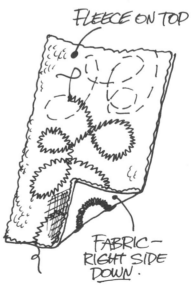

Fig. 4-18 Quilt the top by sewing over the design lines with *Ribbon Floss* in the bobbin.

Serger tips: BEFORE fusing the fabric to the fleece, embellish the fabric using 3-thread flat-locking with *Ribbon Floss* in the upper looper and all-purpose or serger thread in the needle and lower looper. Use a wide, medium-length stitch, testing and adjusting the width and length for the desired look. (You may need to loosen the tension on the looper threaded with *Ribbon Floss* to allow for adequate coverage.) When flatlocking, fold the fabric wrong sides together and serge the fold, allowing the stitches to hang off the edge so the stitching will pull flat.

To serge-embellish the top AFTER fusing the fleece, serge a thread chain to use as decorative cording. Adjust for a narrow, short- to medium-length stitch with *Ribbon Floss* in the upper looper. Tighten all tensions for a tighter thread chain. Mark the desired design on the right side of the fabric. Adjust for a long wide zigzag, using matching thread in the needle. Top-stitch the thread chain to the fused fabric by zigzagging over it on the design lines.

5. Center the embellished rectangle over the top of the brick with the fabric slightly extending over the brick edges. Glue the fabric in place.

6. Center and fuse the fleece onto the wrong side of the gripper fabric. Lightly press the extra fabric to the wrong side over the fleece and edge-stitch. Glue the fleece side to the bottom of the brick.

7. Fold under and glue 3/4" of one end of the braid. Glue the braid around the upper side edges of the brick, beginning and ending at a corner and covering the raw edges of the embellished top. To finish, fold the end 3/4" to the wrong side and butt the ends. (Fig. 4-19)

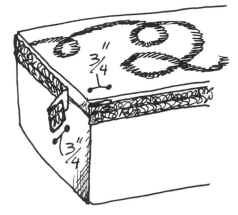

Fig. 4-19 Butt the braid at one corner after turning under the ends.

Decorative Options

♦ Use your serger to embellish the doorstop, following the tips in step 4.

♦ Decorate the brick top with beading, floral appliqués, or hand embroidery instead of *Ribbon Floss*.

ROUNDED COSMETIC BAG

Zip up a simple little bag or create an elegant masterpiece by piecing and/or decoratively stitching the fabric before constructing this handy purse organizer. (Fig. 4-20)

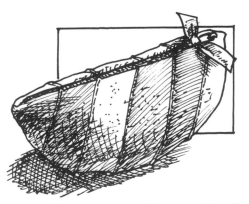

Fig. 4-20 Quickly construct a useful cosmetic bag from embellished fabric.

Materials Needed

♦ 1/6 yard of *Ultrasuede*, other synthetic suede, or another sturdy fabric

♦ 1/6 yard of lightweight lining fabric, such as polyester/cotton or polyester

♦ One 12" or longer matching zipper

♦ 4" of 3/8"-wide ribbon or a 3/8" by 4" strip of *Ultrasuede*

♦ Glue stick

Cutting Directions

♦ Cut two 9" by 6" rectangles from the fabric (either plain fabric or that enhanced by the following decorative options).

♦ Cut two 9" by 6" rectangles from the lining.

♦ Round both corners on one long edge of all the rectangles.

How-Tos

1. Center the right side of the closed zipper on the right side of the long straight edge of one fabric piece, matching the edges. Using a zipper foot, sew a scant 1/8" from the zipper teeth. With the zipper sandwiched between, place a lining straight edge right sides together with the sewn piece and sew over the previous stitching. Press the lining and bag away from the zipper and repeat for the other side of the zipper and the two remaining pieces. Check to be sure the pieces are aligned. (Fig. 4-21)

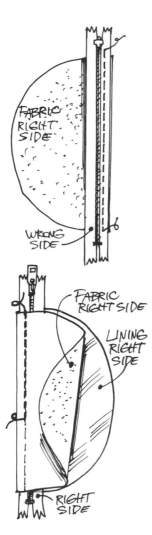

Fig. 4-21 Sew the zipper to one bag and one lining section before repeating on the opposite side.

2. Open the zipper halfway. With the bag right sides together, seam using a 1/4" seam allowance, beginning and ending at the zipper but being careful not to sew into it.

3. Repeat for the lining but taper to a 3/8" seam allowance at the lower rounded edge and leave a 4" opening for turning. Trim the zipper ends to 3/8" and zigzag or serge to finish them. (Fig. 4-22)

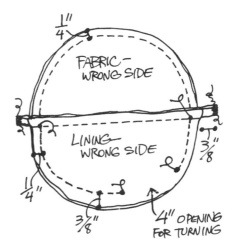

Fig. 4-22 Stitch the fabric and lining sections separately without sewing into the zipper. Finish the zipper ends.

4. Turn the bag right side out. Open the zipper and, beginning at one end, top-stitch on the bag close to the zipper, catching the lining underneath.

5. Press the seam allowances under on the lining opening and top-stitch them closed. Use the ribbon or 3/8"-wide *Ultrasuede* strip for the zipper pull. Taper both ends of the ribbon or strip and thread it through the zipper tab. Tie a knot against the tab to keep the pull in place.

Decorative Options

♦ Before cutting out the bag rectangles when using a soft fabric (such as *Ultrasuede*), use twin-needle top-stitching to create raised tucks. Mark diagonal lines on the fabric 1-1/2" apart. Using a medium to long stitch length, hold the threads taut when starting to sew. Hold the fabric taut in front of and behind the presser foot while sewing. You may need to tighten the needle tension slightly to visibly raise the fabric between the needles.

Serger tip: Use narrow flatlocking instead of twin-needle top-stitching to decorate the diagonal lines. Adjust the serger for a 3-thread flatlock by loosening the needle tension and tightening the lower looper tension. Use buttonhole twist, lightweight pearl cotton, or crochet thread in the upper looper. Flatlock with wrong sides together, allowing the stitches to hang off the edge. For a raised flatlock, tighten the needle tension slightly.

♦ Construct the fabric from 2"-wide strips of *Ultrasuede* or other nonravelly fabric–a good way to use expensive scraps. Overlap the strip long edges 1/4" and glue-baste them together. When dry, top-stitch close to the cut edges using either a straight-stitch or decorative machine stitching. (Fig. 4-23)

Serger tip: Serge-finish the long edges of any fabric strips using decorative thread in the upper looper and a short narrow balanced stitch. Lengthen the stitch slightly and adjust the

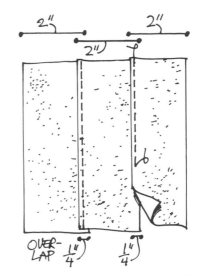

Fig. 4-23 To use scraps instead of fabric yardage, piece overlapped strips.

differential feed (if available) to the lowest setting to prevent the short stitch length from stretching the edge. Lap, glue-baste, and top-stitch the strips as explained above.

RUFFLED SEWING BOX

Give a padded Victorian-look sewing box to any woman on your gift list. It's a great decorative accent for her sewing room but can also double as a hideaway for jewelry, hair ornaments, or mementos. (Fig. 4-24)

Fig. 4-24 Turn a plain round wooden box into a lavish gift with a multitude of uses.

Materials Needed

♦ 1/2 yard of 45"-wide fabric, such as chintz or a cotton print

♦ 1/2 yard of extraloft polyester batting

♦ 1/2 yard of fusible web

♦ Polyester fiberfill

♦ 1/4"-wide satin ribbon three times the box circumference

♦ Filler cord, such as cotton crochet thread or pearl cotton

♦ One round wooden box with a lid–6" to 10" in diameter (available in craft stores)

♦ Glue gun and glue

Cutting Directions

♦ Put the lid on the box. Cut one batting circle with a diameter 1/2" less than the measurement of the box from the lower edge of the lid around the bottom of the box up to the lid on the opposite side. (Fig. 4-25)

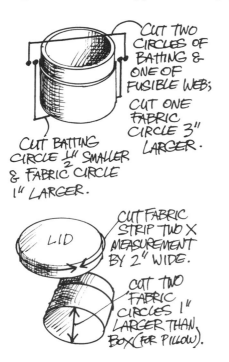

Fig. 4-25 Measure the box accurately before cutting out the fabric and batting.

♦ Cut one fabric circle 1" larger in diameter than the batting circle.

♦ Cut two circles of batting and one circle of fusible web with a diameter equal to the measurement from the lower edge of the lid over the top of the box to the lower lid edge on the opposite side.

♦ Cut one fabric circle 3" larger in diameter than the lid circles.

♦ Cut one ruffle strip (from the fabric) 2" wide by two times the lid circumference.

♦ Cut two fabric circles 1" larger than the box diameter (for the inner pillow).

How-Tos

Sew or serge the seams using 1/4" allowances.

1. With right sides together, seam the two fabric circles for the inner pillow, leaving an opening for turning. Turn the pillow right side out, stuff lightly with fiberfill to form a soft pillow, and hand-sew the opening closed.

Serger tip: Place the circles wrong sides together and serge-seam using a short 3-thread rolled edge, leaving an opening for stuffing. After stuffing, serge-seam the opening closed, overlapping the stitching at both ends. To perfect the rolled edge on the two fabric layers, you may need to widen the stitch, use woolly nylon in the upper looper, and woolly or monofilament nylon in the lower looper.

2. Sandwich the fusible web between the two lid batting circles. Fuse by steaming well, being careful not to flatten the batting. Glue the fused batting to the lid top. Center and glue the larger batting circle around the outside of the box.

3. With right sides together, seam the ruffle strip into a circle.

4. To finish the edges of the ruffle, place filler cord on the right side of each long edge and zigzag over it using a medium-width, medium-length stitch and a contrasting thread color.

5. Adjust to a wider satin-length zigzag stitch and sew over the previous stitching, allowing one side of the stitching to go slightly off the edge of the ruffle. Finish the edges of the two remaining circles using the same technique. (Fig. 4-26)

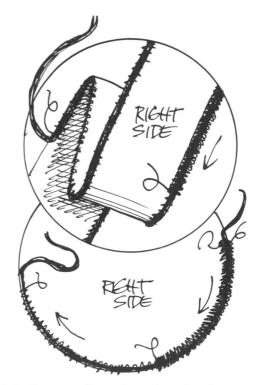

Fig. 4-26 Zigzag cording to the ruffle and circle edges, then cover it with a second layer of satin-length zigzagging.

Serger tip: Finish the edges of the ruffle and the circles using the same rolled-edge settings as described for the pillow.

6. To gather the ruffle and the circles, zigzag over filler cord on the right side, using a long wide stitch and being careful not to catch the cording in the stitching. Position the gathering cord on the ruffle 1/2" from one long edge, on the lid circle 1" from the edge, and on the box circle 1/2" from the finished edge. (Fig. 4-27)

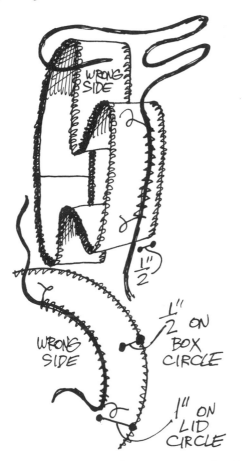

Fig. 4-27 Use filler cord and zigzagging to gather the ruffle and both circles.

7. Place the box circle over the lower part of the box. Pull the filler cord to fit, adjusting the gathers evenly. Knot the cord securely and clip the ends. Glue the fabric to the box under the gathering to hold it in place, enclosing the batting.

8. Glue 1/4"-wide ribbon over the gathering.

9. Place the remaining fabric circle over the lid. Pull the cording to fit, adjust the gathers, knot, and clip the ends. Glue the fabric to the lower edge of the lid, enclosing the batting.

10. Quartermark the lid and the ruffle. Matching the quartermarks, place the wrong side of the ruffle on the right side of the lid, overlapping the hemmed edges 1/2". Pull up the cording to fit, adjust the gathers, knot and clip the cord ends, and glue the ruffle to the lid.

11. Glue ribbon over the gathering stitches on the ruffle, allowing an extra 6" at both ends to tie into a bow. If desired, tie the remaining ribbon into another bow and glue or hand-sew it to the center of the box lid. Place the inner pillow inside the box.

Unique children's gifts are featured in Chapter 2, including a beginner ball for infants, Mr. Tom for children mature enough to use washable markers, and soft fleece slippers for kids of all ages.

Put your sewing skills to work to help celebrate a happy marriage. Chapter 3 includes gifts as simple as a ring bearer's pillow or a lace-trimmed garter, and as elaborate as this ornate wedding-picture frame.

This pretty yet practical lace-trimmed croissant cozy is only one of the novel gifts for women presented in Chapter 4.

Gifts for men and boys are featured in Chapter 5, including this three-way garment bag, which can be used as a hanging clothes bag, a duffle with carrying strap, or a hang-up laundry hamper.

Select gifts for the home and
patio from the eight provided
in Chapter 6. One is this
handy garden tote, which also
functions as a cushioned
kneeling pad.

Country charm is reflected in all the simple gifts from Chapter 7. A lined basket with a padded and appliquéd lid is one of the most elaborate projects included.

From a charming scented soap bag to a handy portable dresser tray, the gifts featured in Chapter 8 are all for use in the bath or boudoir.

Busy people on the go will appreciate the gifts in Chapter 9, including this fold-up glove-compartment organizer to keep small auto accessories conveniently at hand.

CHAPTER FIVE
Gifts for Men and Boys

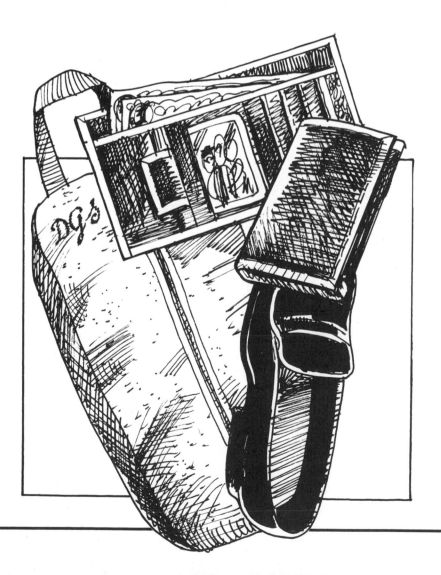

NO-NONSENSE CHEF'S APRON

Make a sensible apron he'll be happy to wear whether he's barbecuing in the backyard or creating a gourmet meal in the kitchen. (Fig. 5-1)

Fig. 5-1 Give your favorite chef a one-size-fits-all apron.

Materials Needed

♦ One yard of 45"-wide or wider mediumweight cotton fabric

Cutting Directions

Refold the fabric and cut out the apron pieces following the pattern measurements. (Fig. 5-2)

How-Tos

1. Fold the apron lengthwise and the pocket cross-wise to press-mark them lightly at the center front. On the sides and lower edge of the pocket rectangle, press a 1/4" hem allowance to the wrong side. At the top edge, fold 1/4" to the wrong side, then press under 1/4" again. From the wrong side, top-stitch close to the hem edge. From the right side, edge-stitch close to the upper fold.

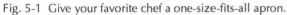

> **Serger tip:** When hemming all edges, serge-finish first, using a wide balanced stitch. Turn the hems to the wrong side and top-stitch them in place.

2. Position the pocket right side up on the right side of the apron in the position indicated on the grid, matching the center-front press-marks. Top-stitch the sides and bottom edge to the apron. Top-stitch again on the center-front line to form two pocket sections.

3. On the top side curves, sides, and lower edge of the apron, press 1/4" to the wrong side and then press 1/4" again. Top-stitch the hems in place.

4. At the upper apron edge, press 1/2" to the wrong side and 1/2" again. Top-stitch close to the hem edge and edge-stitch along the upper edge.

5. On each end of the neck strap, press 1/4" to the wrong side. Then press 1/4" to the wrong side on the long edges. Fold the strap in half lengthwise with wrong sides together, matching the folded edges. Edge-stitch through all layers close to the fold. Repeat for both ties.

> **Serger tip:** Fold the neck strap and ties lengthwise with wrong sides together and serge-finish all four edges of each.

6. Lap the ends of the neck strap 1/2" under each upper front corner of the apron (or lap them on top if they are decoratively serge-finished). Securely top-stitch in a box pattern with diagonal stitching connecting the opposite corners. Repeat for the ties, positioning them outward at both upper side corners.

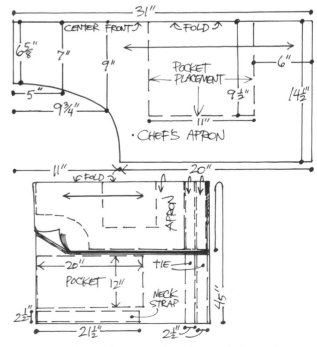

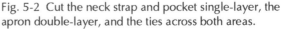

Fig. 5-2 Cut the neck strap and pocket single-layer, the apron double-layer, and the ties across both areas.

ZIPPERED SHOE BAG

Any man will appreciate this handy shoe tote—it's even large enough to carry his running, golf, or other athletic shoes with ease. (Fig. 5-3)

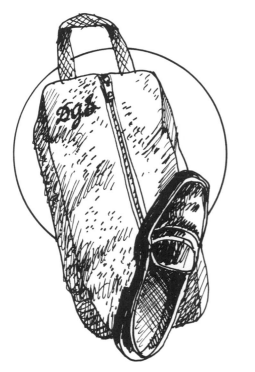

Fig. 5-3 Make him a shoe bag that packs well in a suitcase or acts as a separate tote.

Materials Needed

♦ 1/2 yard of 45"-wide denim, *Ultrasuede,* or nylon pack cloth

♦ One 19" zipper

♦ 1/3 yard of 1"-wide cotton or nylon webbing

Cutting Directions

♦ Cut one 9-1/2" by 17" fabric rectangle for the bag top.

♦ Cut one 9" by 17" fabric rectangle for the bag bottom.

♦ Cut two fabric gussets following the pattern grid. (Fig. 5-4)

How-Tos

Sew or serge all seams using 1/4" allowances.

1. Cut the bag top rectangle in half lengthwise and finish the zipper seam allowance edges using zigzagging, another appropriate machine stitch, or serge-finishing without trimming. Press 1/2" to the wrong side on the finished edges of both rectangles.

2. Lap one folded edge over the top of each side of the zipper, slightly away from the zipper teeth. Match the cut edges on one side of the fabric to the top of the zipper tape. Using a zipper foot, top-stitch the folded edges to the zipper.

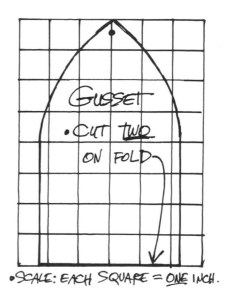

Fig. 5-4 In addition to the bag rectangles, cut two gussets.

3. Position one edge of a gusset against one long edge of the bag front with right sides together. Match the dots to the corner seamlines with the bag front on top and seam from dot to dot. Repeat for the other side of the bag front. (Fig. 5-5)

4. Following the directions in step 3, seam the bag back to the remaining sides of the gussets, sewing just to the dots.

5. Open the zipper at least halfway. With right sides together, seam the lower edge of the bag. Repeat for the upper edge after positioning the webbing ends halfway between the zipper and side edges on both sides with the cut edges matching.

6. Turn the bag right side out.

Decorative Options

♦ Machine-monogram his initials on the bag top before applying the zipper in step 2.

♦ Use a color-matched zipper and webbing to add a decorative accent to a contrasting fabric color.

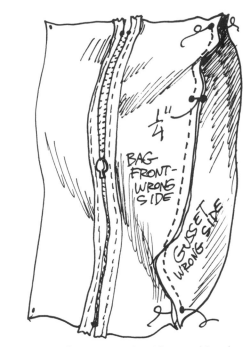

Fig. 5-5 Sew the gusset to the side, matching the corner seamlines to the dots on the underside.

HANGING LOCKER CADDY

For anyone who has a locker at school, work, or an athletic club, this caddy helps solve the dilemma of vertical organization. It hangs on the locker vents and features a mirror plus four handy pockets. (Fig. 5-6)

Fig. 5-6 An easy-to-make locker caddy holds grooming aids and other necessities.

Materials Needed

♦ 1/2 yard of 60"-wide fabric, such as duck or poplin

♦ One 9" zipper

♦ One wire pant hanger (with a cardboard tube at the bottom)

♦ One 6" by 8" (or similar size) lightweight or acrylic mirror

♦ Seam sealant

♦ Glue gun and glue

Cutting Directions

♦ Cut one 10" by 60" fabric rectangle for the caddy.

♦ Cut one 10" by 7-1/2" pocket.

♦ Remove the cardboard tube from the hanger and use pliers to shape the hanger to a 9" width. (Fig. 5-7)

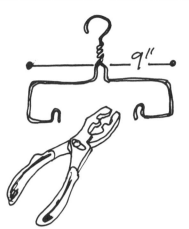

Fig. 5-7 Bend a wire pant hanger to help hold the caddy top rigid and give it a hook for hanging.

How-Tos

Sew or serge the seams using 1/2" allowances.

1. Finish both short ends of the long caddy rectangle using zigzagging, another appropriate machine stitch, or serge-finishing without trimming.

2. Hem one long end of the pocket by pressing 1/2" to the wrong side and then 1/2" again and top-stitching along the hem edge. Press 1/4" to the wrong side on the lower pocket edge. With right sides up, top-stitch the lower pocket edge to the caddy 3" from one short end. Machine-baste the side edges and top-stitch the pocket into thirds. (Fig. 5-8)

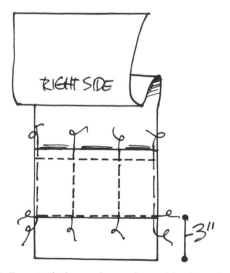

Fig. 5-8 Top-stitch the pocket to the caddy along the lower edge, machine-baste the sides, and top-stitch the pocket dividers.

3. At both short ends of the caddy, press 1/2" to the wrong side. Top-stitch the folded edges to the right side of the zipper, 1/8" from the teeth. Machine-baste the zipper ends together at the seamline on both sides.

4. Fold the caddy circle right sides together to form an 8" zippered pocket at the bottom. (Fig. 5-9)

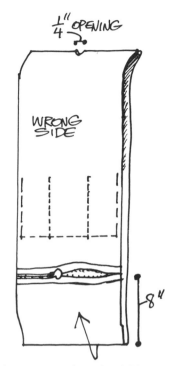

Fig. 5-9 Before seaming the sides, fold a pocket at the lower edge.

5. At the center of the upper edge, trim out a 1/4" circle for the hanger opening. Apply seam sealant and allow it to dry.

6. Open the zipper at least halfway and seam both sides of the entire caddy.

> **Serger tip:** Instead of seaming the sides and turning the caddy right side out, decoratively serge-seam the sides with wrong sides together. Serge-finish the top and bottom edges to match. Apply seam sealant at the corners and clip the threads when dry.

7. Turn the caddy right side out and press. Center the mirror on the front of the caddy 2" below the hanger opening and glue it in place. Insert the hanger through the zippered opening with the hook extending out through the upper caddy edge.

Decorative Options

♦ Before applying the zipper in step 3, machine-monogram his initials in a position to be centered on the lower pocket.

♦ Color-match the pocket and zipper to contrast with the rest of the caddy.

THREE-WAY GARMENT BAG

This versatile clothing tote functions as a garment bag for hanging clothes, a hang-up clothes hamper, and a duffle bag with carrying strap to transport clothes to and from the laundry. (Fig. 5-10)

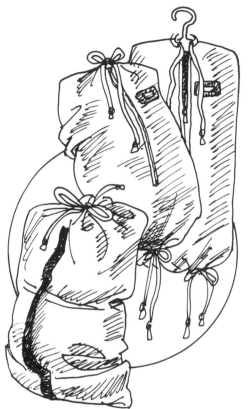

Fig. 5-10 Whether he's at home or on-the-go, he will love this handy garment bag.

Materials Needed

♦ 1-1/2 yards of 60"-wide cotton canvas or denim

♦ One 1-1/2" by 31-1/2" strip of fusible interfacing

♦ 30" of heavy nylon zipper yardage and one zipper pull

♦ 2-1/2 yards of 1/4"-wide cotton cording

♦ 10" of 1/2"-wide single-fold bias tape

♦ One yard of 1"-wide cotton webbing

♦ Glue stick for glue-basting

♦ Removable transparent tape

♦ One large wooden or plastic hanger

Cutting Directions

♦ Cut two 26" by 46" canvas rectangles.

♦ With the rectangles right sides together, trace around a large plastic or wooden hanger to shape the upper bag edge. Cut on the traced lines.

♦ Curve out the center of the top edges for the hanger opening. (Fig. 5-11)

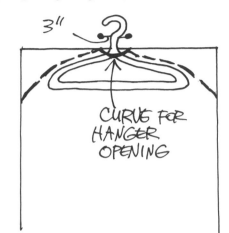

Fig. 5-11 Trace around the top of a hanger to shape the bag top.

How-Tos

Sew or serge all seams using 1/2" seam allowances. Finish straight-stitched allowances by zigzagging the edges.

1. For the bag front, fold and press one rectangle in half lengthwise. Center the strip of fusible interfacing on the press-mark beginning at the curved edge. Fuse it in place and press-mark again. Using a disappearing marker, draw a line on the press-mark from the upper edge down 30-1/2". Using a short stitch length, stay-stitch 1/4" from the line on both sides and across the bottom, forming a rectangle. Cut on the line, angling into the lower corners but being careful not to cut into the stitching. (Fig. 5-12)

> **Serger tip:** After cutting the rectangular opening, stabilize the cut edges by serge-finishing them, using a medium- to narrow-width, balanced 3-thread stitch.

2. Press the opening edges to the wrong side on the stay-stitching lines. Center the opening over the right side of the zipper 1/8" from the zipper teeth. Hold the zipper in place for application with transparent tape on the reverse side. Using a zipper foot, top-stitch the folds next to the zipper from the right side.

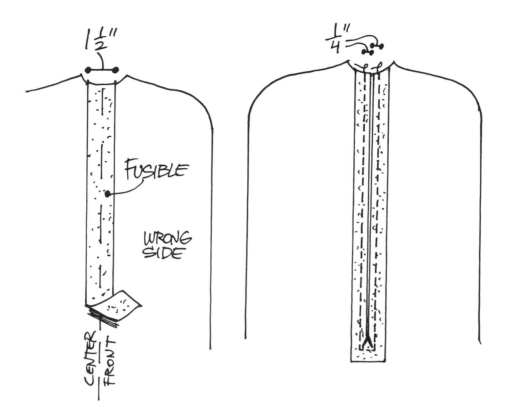

Fig. 5-12 Stay-stitch and cut a rectangular opening to be layered and top-stitched over the zipper.

3. Press-mark the center-back line, wrong sides together, on the other rectangle.

4. Fold and glue-baste 1" to the wrong side on both ends of the webbing strip. After drying, position the wrong side of the strap vertically on the right side of the bag center back, beginning 1" from the upper edge. Top-stitch a box over both ends to secure it. Top-stitch another box 9" from the upper strap edge to form a carrying handle. Reinforce the boxes with diagonal rows of stitching connecting the opposite corners.

5. With the bag right sides together, seam the sides and around to the upper hanger opening. Turn the bag right side out.

6. On the right-side lower edge of the bag, mark and sew two 1/2"-long buttonholes for the drawstring openings. Position them on either side of the seamline, parallel to it and 3/4" away, beginning 1-1/2" from the cut edge. (Fig. 5-13)

7. At the lower edge, press 1/4" to the wrong side and press 1" again. Top-stitch the hem into position, forming a casing.

> **Serger tip:** Serge-finish the lower edge using a medium-width 3-thread stitch, trimming 1/4". Turn and top-stitch a 1" hem.

8. Fold both ends of the bias binding 1/2" to the wrong side and bind the hanger opening on the upper edge, butting the ends. Cut a 22"-long piece of cording and thread it through the binding. Thread the other piece of cording through the buttonholes and hem casing at the lower edge. Knot the cording ends securely.

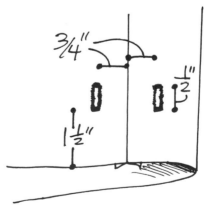

Fig. 5-13 Stitch two buttonholes near the lower edge for the drawstring.

Decorative Options

♦ Color-match the zipper, bias tape, and cotton webbing for an interesting accent or use black fabric with multicolored bright accents.

♦ Make a holder for an identification tag or business card from two 2-1/2" by 5-1/2" pieces of *Ultrasuede*. With wrong sides together, use glue stick to glue-baste the two pieces together. Then cut a rectangle out of the center 1/2" away from the long edges and 1-1/4" away from the ends. Glue-baste a 2-1/2" by 5-1/2" piece of clear acrylic or clear lightweight vinyl to the back of the holder. Round all corners. Use transparent tape to position the tag holder on the right side of the bag front approximately 11" from the upper edge and 2" from the center-front zipper position. Top-stitch the holder into position, leaving the right end open for inserting the tag or card. (Fig. 5-14)

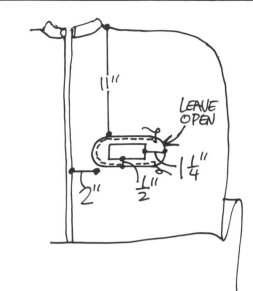

Fig. 5-14 Use a small scrap of *Ultrasuede* and see-through acrylic or vinyl to make an identification holder.

ROLL-UP STADIUM SEAT

The perfect gift for any sports fan, this soft carry-along cushion is lightweight, washable, and works on all types of stadium seats. It can be a strapped-on seat back and cushion for one person or a seat cushion for either one or two. (Fig. 5-15)

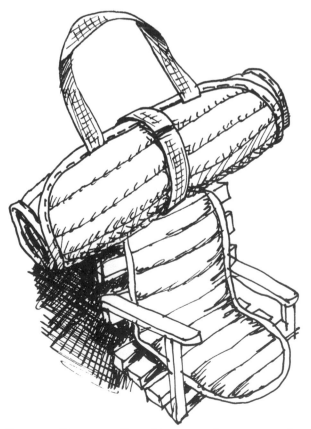

Fig. 5-15 Give a versatile cushion to comfort any sports fan.

Materials Needed

♦ 7/8 yard of heavy polyester fleece, such as polar fleece

♦ 1/2 yard of fusible fleece

♦ 7/8 yard of 1"-wide cotton or nylon webbing

♦ 2-2/3 yards of 1"-wide grosgrain ribbon or extra-wide double-fold bias tape

♦ 1" of 1-1/2"-wide *Velcro*

Cutting Directions

♦ Cut one 34" by 28" polyester fleece rectangle.

♦ Cut one 34" by 14" fusible fleece rectangle.

How-Tos

1. Position the fusible fleece on the wrong side of half the polyester fleece rectangle. Fuse it in place.

2. Fold the polyester fleece wrong sides together over the fusible fleece and pin securely.

3. Using a long stitch, sew crosswise parallel lines 1-1/2" apart to quilt the rectangle. Trim the rectangle to 32" by 14".

4. Using a saucer as a guide, round all four corners. Zigzag, using a long stitch close to all edges to compress the layers for binding.

5. Cut the webbing into two equal lengths. On one piece, top-stitch the looped side of the *Velcro* 1" from one end. Lap the hooked side of the *Velcro* 1/4" over the other end and top-stitch. Fold the *Velcro,* along with the overlapped webbing, to the underside and top-stitch around all four edges. (Fig. 5-16)

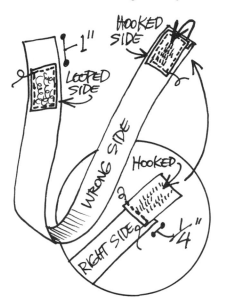

Fig. 5-16 Prepare half the webbing by sewing on pieces of *Velcro.*

6. Pin the webbing with *Velcro* in the center of one short end of the cushion with the cut edges matching and the looped side up. On the same end, match and pin the cut edges of the other webbing strip 2" on either side of the first webbing. (Fig. 5-17)

7. Press the ribbon exactly in half lengthwise. Beginning at the middle of the end opposite the straps, fold the ribbon tightly over the cut edges and top-stitch the ribbon edge around the cushion, making certain to catch the ribbon underlayer in the stitching. At the end, fold 3/8" of the ribbon to the wrong side and lap it 1/2" over the beginning end. **Optional:** Use bias binding instead of grosgrain ribbon to bind the edges, following the same technique.

8. Roll up the cushion from the end without the straps, securing the *Velcro* webbing around the center.

Decorative Options

♦ Use the colors of his favorite sports team for the fleece, binding, and webbing.

♦ Purchase and hand-sew an official team logo on the outside of the rolled-up seat.

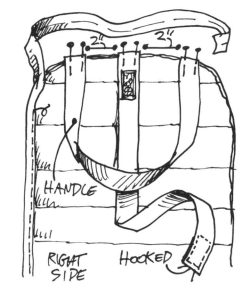

Fig. 5-17 Position the webbing at one short end so it will be attached with the binding.

COMPUTER-DISC CARRIER

Your favorite computer buff can carry nine 3-1/2" discs in this sturdy and compact case. It also works well as an organizer for a baseball card collector. (Fig. 5-18)

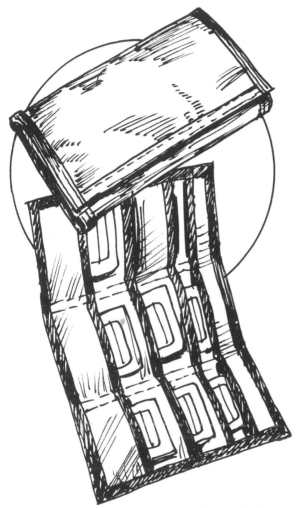

Fig. 5-18 Delight your computer wizard or baseball card collector with a carrying case organizer.

Materials Needed

♦ 1/3 yard of 60"-wide nylon pack cloth

♦ 3-1/3 yards of 5/8"-wide grosgrain ribbon

♦ 10" of 3/4"-wide *Velcro*

♦ **Optional:** Glue stick

Cutting Directions

♦ Cut two 15" by 10" pack cloth rectangles for the carrier front and back.

♦ Cut three 15" by 3-1/4" pack cloth rectangles for the disc pockets.

♦ Cut one 15" by 1-1/2" pack cloth rectangle for the upper flap.

How-Tos

When top-stitching and edge-stitching the grosgrain ribbon, use a long (8 stitches per inch) straight-stitch.

1. Press approximately 18" of the grosgrain ribbon exactly in half lengthwise. Fold the ribbon over one long edge of one 15" by 3-1/4" pocket rectangles with the raw edge of the fabric against the fold of the ribbon. From the right side of the fabric, top-stitch the ribbon in place close to its edge, being careful to catch the underside of the ribbon in the stitching. Edge-stitch again close to the fold of the ribbon. Repeat for the other 15" by 3-1/4" pocket rectangles and the 1-1/2"-wide flap rectangle.

> **Serger tip:** Use a heavy decorative thread (such as pearl cotton or crochet thread) in the upper looper and serge-finish the pocket and flap edges using a wide, satin-length, balanced 3-thread stitch instead of binding them.

2. Place one 15" by 3-1/4" pocket rectangle on one of the carrier rectangles, wrong sides together, with the bound edge 2-1/4" below one long edge. Top-stitch 1/4" from the long raw edge of the pocket. (Fig. 5-19)

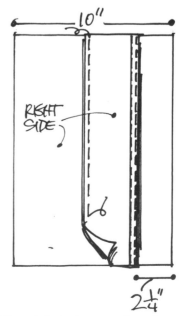

Fig. 5-19 Top-stitch the lower pocket edge to the carrier rectangle.

3. With wrong sides together, place another pocket rectangle on the carrier rectangle, lapping the bound edge 1" over the raw edge of the previous pocket. Top-stitch 1/4" from the long cut edge. Repeat for the remaining pocket.

4. To form smaller pockets, top-stitch two parallel lines 4" and 4-5/8" from the right side of the carrier rectangle. Top-stitch two other parallel lines 5" and 5-7/8" from the left side of the carrier.

5. With wrong sides together and matching the cut edges, place the narrow flap rectangle on the top of the carrier. Machine-baste close to the cut edges.

6. Place the rougher hook side of the *Velcro* strip over the pockets on the left side of the carrier, matching the edges. Top-stitch both long edges of the *Velcro* in place.

7. On the right side of the fabric on the other carrier rectangle, top-stitch the loop *Velcro* strip parallel to and 3-1/2" from the left side.

8. Place the carrier front and back wrong sides together. Using a medium-length and medium-width zigzag, machine-baste around the entire carrier.

9. Press the remaining ribbon exactly in half lengthwise. With the pockets up, bind the edges with the ribbon starting at the lower-left corner. Top-stitch the ribbon in place, catching both long edges, until you reach the end of the next corner. Remove the project from the machine and fold the ribbon to miter the corners on both the upper and under sides. (Fig. 5-20)

10. Beginning at the mitered corner, top-stitch the ribbon to the remaining sides, repeating the corner mitering. When you reach the beginning bound corner, fold 3/8" of the ribbon to the wrong side and lap it over the beginning end. (For ease in finishing the corner, you may want to glue the folded ribbon into position before lapping.) Then edge-stitch the entire carrier close to the folded ribbon edge.

> **Serger tip:** Serge-finish the four outer edges to match the pockets (instead of binding them), using the decorative thread in both loopers. Apply seam sealant at the corners and clip the threads when dry.

11. Fold the carrier twice vertically near the double rows of stitching and close it with the *Velcro*.

Decorative Options

♦ Use contrasting colors of pack cloth and ribbon (red, white, and blue, for example) for more interest.

♦ Color-coordinate the baseball card collector's carrier to his favorite team's colors.

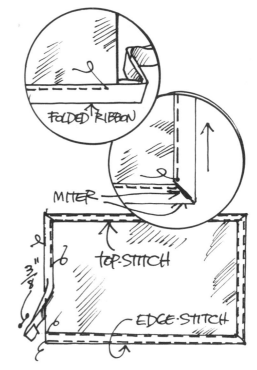

Fig. 5-20 Miter each corner before reinserting the binding under the needle and continuing to top-stitch the edges, lapping the final end. Then edge-stitch all four sides.

ULTRASUEDE TIE CASE

His ties will stay neat and wrinkle-free when he travels using this special zippered case. Three elastic strips on both sides hold four to six ties in place. (Fig. 5-21)

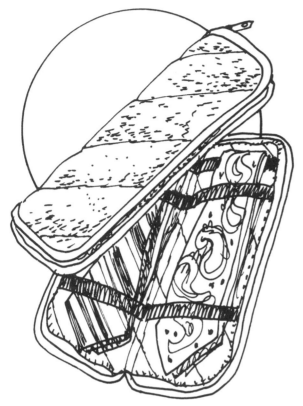

Fig. 5-21 Any man who wears ties can use this nifty travel case.

Materials Needed

♦ One 13" by 17" piece of *Ultrasuede*

♦ One 13" by 17" piece of heavy fusible interfacing

♦ One 13" by 17" piece of fusible fleece

♦ One 15" by 19" piece of polyester or rayon lining fabric

♦ 2/3 yard of 1"-wide elastic

♦ 1/3 yard of 1/2"- or 3/4"-wide elastic

♦ 30" of zipper yardage with one zipper pull

♦ 1-3/4 yards of 3/4"-wide grosgrain ribbon

Cutting Directions

Cut the materials needed to the exact dimensions listed above.

How-Tos

1. Fuse the interfacing to the wrong side of the *Ultrasuede*. Fuse the piece of fleece to the interfacing side of the *Ultrasuede*.

2. Center the wrong side of the lining over the fleece side of the *Ultrasuede*. Pin securely. From the lining side, quilt through all layers, using a long stitch and parallel diagonal rows approximately 2" apart. Trim the lining to fit.

3. With wrong sides together, fold the case in half lengthwise. Round all four corners.

4. Using an air-erasable marker, draw a line on the lining side marking the lengthwise center of the case.

5. Cut the 1"-wide elastic into two 12" pieces and mark the center of each. Matching the elastic markings and the center marking on the case, pin one elastic piece to the lining side of the case 3-1/2" from the bottom and the other 11-1/2" from the bottom. Mark the center of the narrower elastic and pin it to the case center marking 1" from the top. From the lining side, top-stitch through all layers 1/4" away from the center marking on both sides. (Fig. 5-22)

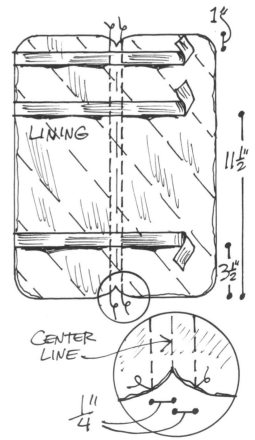

Fig. 5-22 Anchor the elastic strips with two rows of top-stitching down the center of the case.

6. Stretch and pin the elastic ends horizontally across to the edges of the case. Using a narrow zigzag, machine-baste around all the edges, catching the elastic in the stitching.

7. Beginning at the center top and matching the edges, place the wrong side of the opened zipper against the right side of the lining. Taper the ends of the zipper tape and ease the zipper around the corners. Machine-baste the zipper around the case using a narrow zigzag. (Fig. 5-23)

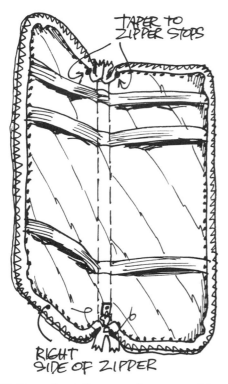

Fig. 5-23 Zigzag-baste the open zipper around the edges of the case.

8. Press the grosgrain ribbon exactly in half lengthwise. Beginning at the center top, fold the ribbon tightly over the edge of the case. Top-stitch close to the ribbon edge, easing around the corners and making sure to catch the underlayer of ribbon in the stitching. To end, fold 3/8" of the ribbon to the wrong side and lap it over the beginning end for 3/8". (Fig. 5-24)

Fig. 5-24 Fold and lap the end of the binding at the center top of the case.

Decorative Options

♦ Color-coordinate the tie case with the previous shoe bag for a double-special gift.

♦ Quilt the case in step 2 using a contrasting decorative thread in the bobbin.

DUAL-FOLD WALLET

This tough little nylon wallet will last for years. It contains handy pockets for bills, credit cards, business cards, photos, and coins and seals closed with a strip of Velcro. *(Fig. 5-25)*

Fig. 5-25 Adapted from a popular wallet design, this gift can keep anyone organized.

Materials Needed

♦ 1/6 yard of nylon pack cloth

♦ One 10" by 6" piece of matching lining fabric

♦ One 10" by 6" piece of lightweight fleece

♦ 5-1/2" of 3/4"-wide *Velcro*

♦ 1-1/2 yards of 5/8"-wide grosgrain ribbon

♦ **Optional:** Plastic photo windows

Cutting Directions

From the pack cloth:

♦ Cut one 9-1/2" by 5" rectangle for the wallet back.

♦ Cut one 9-1/2" by 4-1/2" rectangle for the wallet front.

♦ Cut three 2-1/2" by 4-1/2" credit-card pockets.

♦ Cut one 3-3/4" by 4-1/2" pocket.

♦ Cut one 5-1/2" by 4-1/2" rectangle for a folded double pocket.

♦ Cut one 6-1/2" by 4-1/2" rectangle for the coin pocket.

♦ Cut one 3-1/4" square for the coin pocket flap.

From the lining and fleece:

♦ Cut one 9-1/2" by 4-1/2" rectangle of each.

How-Tos

1. On the three credit-card pockets and the 3-3/4" pocket, turn one long edge 1/2" to the wrong side and edge-stitch along the fold.

2. Place one of the credit-card pockets right side up on the right side of the 3-3/4" pocket with the finished edges 3/8" apart. Top-stitch the credit-card pocket to the larger pocket 1/4" from the long unfinished edge. Repeat for one other credit-card pocket, positioning the finished edge 3/8" from the previous pocket's finished edge. (Fig. 5-26)

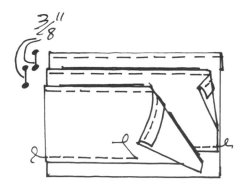

Fig. 5-26 Top-stitch two credit-card pockets to the 3-3/4" pocket.

3. Cut a 4-1/2" strip of the *Velcro*. Top-stitch the wrong side of the hooked portion of the *Velcro* to the right side of the remaining credit-card pocket's long unfinished edge.

4. With both right sides up, place the layered pockets on the right end of the wallet front, matching the cut edges. Place the *Velcro*-trimmed pocket right side up on top of the other layered pockets, again matching the cut edges. Machine-baste the cut edges of the pockets to the wallet front, stitching through all layers 1/4" from the edges.

5. For the folded double pocket, press under 1/2" on one short end and edge-stitch. Fold the pocket crosswise, wrong sides together, so the hemmed side is slightly longer than the unhemmed side. Edge-stitch along the fold. Place the pocket on the wallet front with the unfinished vertical edge down and 1/2" away from the nearest pocket. Top-stitch 1/4" from the unfinished edge, holding the finished edge out of the way of the stitching. Machine-baste the horizontal edges into position 1/4" from the top and bottom. (Fig. 5-27)

6. On one short end of the coin-pocket rectangle, fold 1/2" to the wrong side and edge-stitch. Center and top-stitch the looped side of the remaining 1" of *Velcro* along the fold on the right side. Press the other short end of the rectangle 1/2" to the right side.

7. To form the coin pocket, fold the rectangle crosswise, wrong sides together, with the *Velcro* portion on top and 2-1/2" deep. Matching the pocket fold to the unfinished short end of the wallet front, machine-baste 1/4" from the three outside edges. (Fig. 5-28)

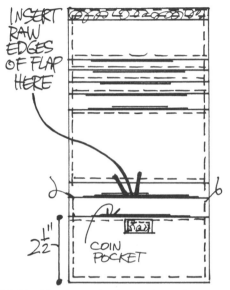

Fig. 5-28 Machine-baste the three edges of the coin pocket to the wallet front before preparing and attaching the flap.

8. Fold the coin pocket flap in half with wrong sides together. Center and top-stitch the hooked side of the 1" *Velcro* along the fold.

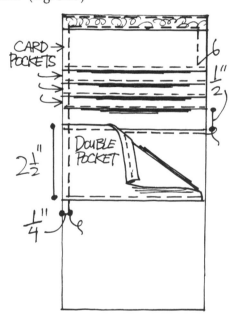

Fig. 5-27 After top-stitching the unfinished edge of the double pocket to the wallet front, machine-baste the upper and lower edges through all layers.

9. Press approximately 10" of the ribbon exactly in half lengthwise. Bind the two sides and the folded edge of the flap with the ribbon. Use the mitering method described in steps 9 and 10 of the Computer-disc Carrier or use separate ribbon sections for each edge to be bound, turning under 3/8" when lapping the corners. (Fig. 5-29)

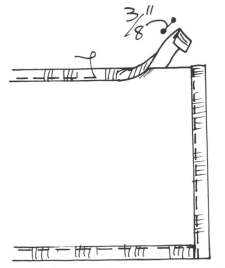

Fig. 5-29 Instead of mitering the corners, you may choose to fold under and lap the ends of separate binding sections at each corner.

10. With the *Velcro* side up, center and insert the flap cut edges 1/2" inside the unstitched folded edge of the coin pocket. Fold the flap down and top-stitch through all layers across the entire folded edge.

11. Fold a 9-1/2" section of ribbon exactly in half lengthwise and bind the upper edge of the wallet front, leaving the ends unfinished.

12. On the right side of the wallet back, center and top-stitch the remaining looped *Velcro* strip parallel to and 1-3/4" away from one short end.

13. Machine-baste the lining and the wallet back wrong sides together with the fleece sandwiched between. Place the wallet back and front wrong sides together with the *Velcro* end of the back positioned on the underside of the coin pocket. Match and machine-baste the sides and lower edges.

14. Press the remaining ribbon exactly in half lengthwise. With the wallet front up, begin binding all four outer edges, starting at the lower-left corner. Use either the folded-and-lapped corner technique described in step 9 or the mitered-corner method featured in steps 9 and 10 of the Computer-disc Carrier. (Fig. 5-30)

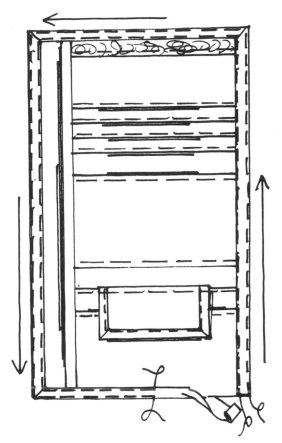

Fig. 5-30 Bind the outer edges of the wallet.

15. Insert the plastic photo windows into one side of the folded pocket, fold the wallet in thirds vertically, and seal it closed with the *Velcro*.

Decorative Options

♦ Match the grosgrain ribbon to the pack cloth for a subtle effect or use contrasting colors for added interest.

♦ After completing step 11, machine-monogram his initials on the wallet back opposite the *Velcro* strip.

CHAPTER SIX
Gifts for the Home and Patio

DECORATOR GUEST TOWELS

Although these quick and easy towels make a much appreciated hostess gift, you'll probably want to treat yourself to some as well. They're a perfect way to show off your sewing skills. (Fig. 6-1)

Fig. 6-1 Feature a Battenberg lace motif on each towel.

Materials Needed

♦ Purchased linen or cotton guest towels (or use 1-1/4 yards of 45"-wide linen or cotton to make six towels)

♦ Battenberg lace motifs (one for each towel) narrower than the towel ends

Cutting Directions

To make the towels, cut each one 15" by 23", using the selvage for one short edge.

How-Tos

1. If you're making the towels, press 1/4" to the wrong side on both long edges. Edge-stitch along the fold. Press under 1/4" again and top-stitch over the previous stitching. Repeat for the unfinished short end.

> **Serger tip:** Serge-finish the edges without trimming, using a wide, medium-length 3- or 3/4-thread stitch. Fold the fabric under on the needleline and fold again. (The wide serger stitch is approximately 1/4" and will help you turn the hems neatly and easily.) Then top-stitch close to the hem edge.

2. On the selvage end of the towel, center the Battenberg motif and zigzag top-stitch all but the bottom edge to the towel using a narrow medium-length stitch. (Fig. 6-2)

Fig. 6-2 Apply the motif with narrow zigzagging, trim away the fabric underneath, and zigzag again.

3. Carefully trim the fabric away from the underside. Zigzag around the edge of the motif, over the original stitching, using a wider satin-length stitch to finish the application.

4. Machine-embroider a monogram above the motif.

Decorative Options

♦ Appliqué, machine-embroider, or hand-embroider any appropriate design on the towels instead of using the Battenberg lace.

♦ Use your serger to decorate the towels. Possibilities include diagonal parallel rows of flatlocking, decorative serge-finished edges, and serge-finished appliqués.

UMBRELLA-TABLE COVER

Anyone with a round umbrella table will enjoy this bright and cheery tablecloth that fits a 42" to 60" diameter table. It features a center hole for the umbrella pole and a Velcro closure for easy on and off. (Fig. 6-3)

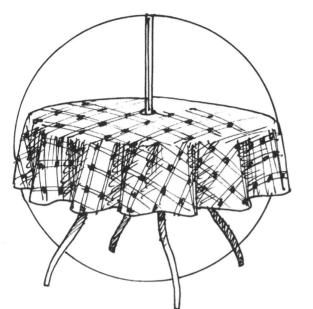

Fig. 6-3 Make the table cover from vinyl and you won't need to hem it.

Materials Needed

♦ 3 yards of 54"-wide heavy fabric, such as flannel-backed vinyl, cotton duck, or sailcloth (or purchase 2-1/2 yards of 60"-wide fabric or 2 yards of 72"-wide fabric)

♦ One yard of 3/4"-wide *Velcro*

♦ One 72" by 36" rectangle of tracing material

Cutting Directions

♦ Fold the tracing material in half crosswise. Using a measuring tape pivoted from point A, mark lines 3/4" and 35-1/4" away. Cut on the marked lines. (Fig. 6-4)

♦ Place the pattern lengthwise on the fabric with the straight edges 1" from the selvages and cut out the two pieces.

How-Tos

Seam or top-stitch vinyl fabric using a long (8 stitches per inch) straight-stitch.

1. Seam one side of the semicircle's center line, right sides together, using a 1" allowance. Finger-press the seam open and top-stitch 1/4" on both sides of the seamline. Trim the excess allowance close to the top-stitching.

Serger tip: Serge-seam the cover instead, trimming 3/4". Then press the allowance to one side and top-stitch over it.

2. When using woven fabric, press 1/4" to the wrong side on the outer edge of the circle and edge-stitch along the fold. (You can leave vinyl unhemmed.) Press under 1/4" again and top-stitch over the previous stitching.

Serger tip: Serge-finish the edge before hemming it using a medium- to wide-width balanced stitch. Turn the serged edge to the wrong side along the needleline and top-stitch it in place.

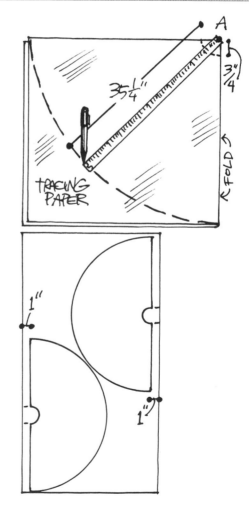

Fig. 6-4 Draw a pattern on tracing paper and add seam allowances when cutting out the fabric.

3. On the inner circle, fold the cut edges 1/8" to the wrong side and edge-stitch along the fold. Trim the allowance close to the stitching.

> **Serger tip:** Serge-finish the inner circle edge using a narrow, medium- to short-length, balanced 3-thread stitch and trimming 1/8". Test first and lengthen the stitch slightly to avoid ruffling the edge.

4. Attach the *Velcro* closure to the remaining unstitched edges. Place the hooked *Velcro* section on the left-hand side of the opening, both right side up, matching the edges. Top-stitch the left side of the strip to the fabric and trim the allowance to 1/4" from the stitching. Turn the *Velcro* to the underside and top-stitch it into position along its other edge. (Fig. 6-5)

5. Working from the underside, on the right-hand side of the opening, lap the looped section of the *Velcro,* right side up, 1/4" over the wrong side of the edge and top-stitch. Wrap the *Velcro* to the right side of the fabric and top-stitch its remaining edge.

6. Seal the two *Velcro* sections, beginning at the center of the cover, so the table cover forms a complete circle.

Decorative Options

♦ On a solid-color table cover, machine-embroider a design around the outer edge, 3" from the hem.

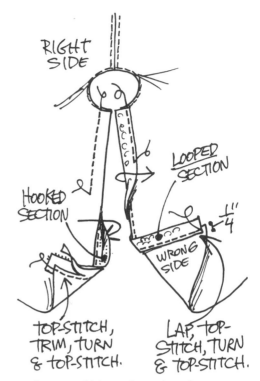

Fig. 6-5 Sew on a *Velcro* strip to close the cover.

♦ Use same-size layers of fabric, fusible fleece, and backing material. Fuse the fleece to the wrong side of the fabric and place the backing on the fleece side. Quilt through all layers from the right side, using intersecting parallel rows of stitching or echo quilting around a design on the fabric. Handle the quilted fabric as one layer when following the project instructions.

REMOVABLE BASKET LINERS

Dress up a set of baskets for a useful gift that adds a charming touch to picnics and casual dining. Choose from two styles—one ties on over a basket's handles and the other is held in place by an elasticized hem. Both remove easily for washing. (Fig. 6-6)

Fig. 6-6 Turn plain baskets into great gifts.

Materials Needed

♦ One remnant of woven cotton fabric, such as gingham or terry, 4" greater in width and length than the basket's inner dimensions

♦ One piece of 1/4"-wide braided elastic, 2" less than the circumference of the basket's upper edge

♦ For a basket without a handle: Extrawide double-fold bias tape equal in length to the circumference of the basket's upper edge

♦ For a basket with a handle: Extrawide double-fold bias tape equal in length to the circumference of the basket's upper edge plus 1-3/4 yards

Cutting Directions

♦ Measure the inside of the basket from the top edge, down one side, across the bottom, and up the opposite side and add 4". Repeat the measurements in the opposite direction. Cut the liner to these

measurements. Then, using the upper edge of the basket as a guide, curve the corners of the fabric. (Fig. 6-7)

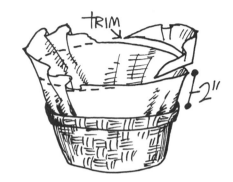

Fig. 6-7 Center the liner in the basket and trim to even the edges.

♦ For a basket with a handle, place the liner fabric inside the basket and mark the handle positions. Cut out 4" openings the width of the handles. (Fig. 6-8)

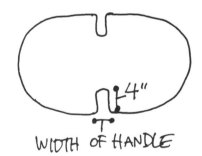

Fig. 6-8 Allow space for the basket handles.

How-Tos

To line a basket without a handle:

1. Bind the liner edges, folding both ends of the binding 1/2" to the wrong side and butting them together, leaving an opening to insert the elastic.

2. Using a safety pin or bodkin, thread the elastic through the binding casing. Overlap the elastic ends and sew them securely together before hiding them inside the casing. Hand-sew the binding ends together, if desired. Place the liner into the basket, folding the elastic hem approximately 2" over the edge.

To line a basket with a handle:

1. Bind the handle openings using the bias tape. Repeat for the outer edges, folding the binding 1/2" to the wrong side at the beginning and ending of each handle opening, leaving the ends open for inserting the elastic.

2. Cut the remaining binding into four equal lengths for the ties and cut the elastic into two equal lengths. On each end of the two elastic sections, lap a piece of the binding 3/8" over it, folding the binding in half again with the elastic sandwiched in the middle. Sew securely across the joined ends and edge-stitch the binding edges together. (Fig. 6-9)

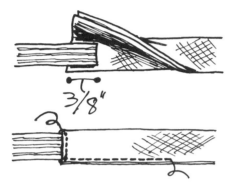

Fig. 6-9 Lap the elastic over the binding, fold the binding again, sew them together, and edge-stitch the binding.

3. Using a safety pin or bodkin, thread the elastic and ties through the casing. With the seams of the elastic and ties 1/4" inside the casing, sew across each casing end to hold them in position.

4. Knot the end of each tie. Place the liner into the basket and tie it around the handle on both sides.

Decorative Options

♦ Embellish the fabric with decorative machine stitching or serging before cutting out the liners.

♦ Make bias tape from fabric to match the liners (especially effective for a check or stripe where the bias grain will be evident). Cut a bias strip 2" wide and press three equidistant folds so the folded strip is 1/2" wide. (Fig. 6-10)

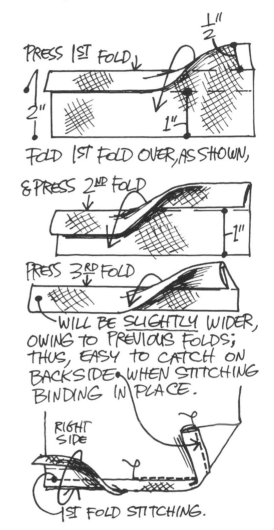

Fig. 6-10 Make double-fold bias tape to bind the liner edges.

MUSHROOM AND LETTUCE CRISPERS

Fragile produce will stay fresh longer when stored in these practical but pretty bags. Make them in two sizes for mushrooms and lettuce. Constructed of 100% cotton, they're easy to keep damp so the vegetables will stay crisp and they're also washable. (Fig. 6-11)

Fig. 6-11 Any salad lover on your gift list will put these veggie keepers to good use.

Materials Needed

♦ 1/2 yard of 35"-wide or wider mediumweight 100% cotton fabric, such as ticking, for the lettuce keeper, and an additional 1/4 yard for the mushroom keeper

♦ Four yards of double-fold bias tape

♦ Fabric paint in a contrasting color

Cutting Directions

♦ Cut one 35" by 13" rectangle for the lettuce keeper.

♦ Cut one 24" by 9" rectangle for the mushroom keeper.

♦ Cut one 3-1/2" by 13" rectangle and one 3-1/2" by 9" rectangle for the band closures that hold the flap.

How-Tos

1. Round one short end of both large rectangles.

2. Fold both bands in half lengthwise, right sides together, and seam the long cut edges using a 1/4" seam allowance. Turn them right side out and press carefully, centering the seams on the back side of the bands.

> **Serger tip:** To avoid turning the bands, fold them in half lengthwise, wrong sides together, and serge-seam. Press as described above to hide the stitching.

3. Bind the straight short end on both rectangles. With wrong sides together, press up 14" on the lettuce keeper and 10" on the mushroom keeper to mark the pockets.

> **Serger tip:** Decoratively serge-finish the straight edges instead of binding them. Use a wide, satin-length, balanced 3- or 3/4-thread stitch and decorative washable thread, such as pearl cotton or cotton crochet thread, in both loopers. You may also choose to decoratively serge-finish the long edges of the bands in step 2 to match.

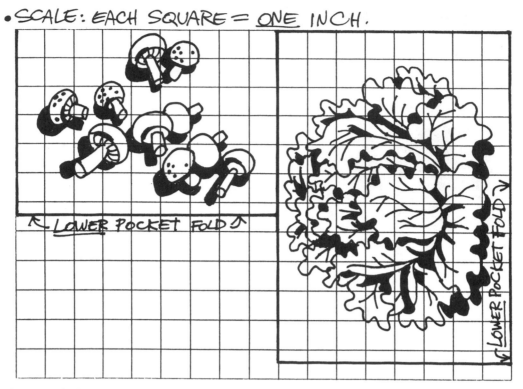

Fig. 6-12 Use these simple designs or draw something more elaborate.

4. Unfold the bag. Center and paint the mushroom design on the pocket section of the smaller bag and the lettuce design on the larger one, following the pattern grid. (Fig. 6-12)

5. Place the wider band on the lettuce keeper 2" from the bound edge with the seam down and cut edges matching. Place the other band on the mushroom keeper 1" from the bound edge.

6. Fold 1/2" to the wrong side on one end of the binding. Bind the remaining cut edges of the bag, beginning at one lower corner and ending at the other, turning under another 1/2" to finish. (Fig. 6-13)

> **Serger tip:** Serge-finish the outer edge to match the previous stitching. Use seam sealant on the lower corners and clip the threads when dry.

7. On both bags, tuck the rounded flap under the band to close the crisper.

Decorative Options

♦ Appliqué or machine-embroider decorative designs on the crispers instead of using fabric paint.

♦ Select a print fabric with a vegetable motif for the speediest alternative.

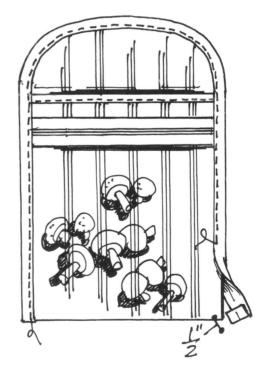

Fig. 6-13 Apply binding around the bag and flap.

INSULATED BAKER'S GLOVES

Modeled after gloves worn by professional bakers, this helpful gift gives the recipient full protection from painful burns when reaching into a hot oven. (Fig. 6-14)

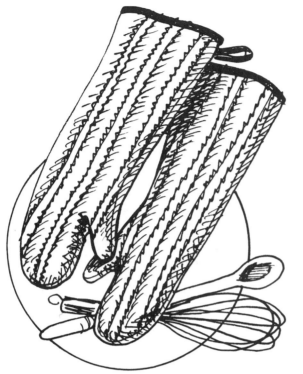

Fig. 6-14 Give a pair of baker's gloves to your favorite cook.

Materials Needed

♦ 1/2 yard of heavy woven cotton, such as denim or duck

♦ 1/2 yard of fusible polyester fleece

♦ 1/2 yard of insulating material, such as a *Teflon*-coated fabric, for the glove lining

Cutting Directions

♦ Prepare the fabric for quilting by fusing the fleece to the lining wrong side. Place the wrong sides of the cotton fabric and fleece together. Quilt the fabric from the right side, using a long (8 stitches per inch) straight-stitch and parallel rows. If the fabric has stripes or vertical design lines, use those as a guide.

♦ Cut four gloves from the quilted fabric, using the grid and flipping the pattern for the glove backs. (Fig. 6-15)

♦ Cut one 1-1/2" by 12" matching cotton fabric strip for the loops.

♦ Cut two 2" by 16" matching cotton fabric strips for the binding.

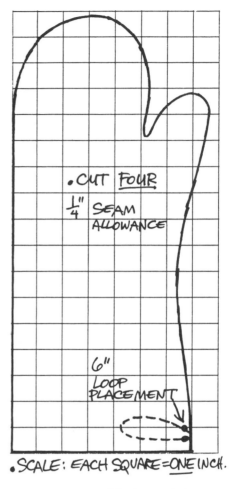

CUT FOUR
1/4" SEAM ALLOWANCE

6" LOOP PLACEMENT

SCALE: EACH SQUARE = ONE INCH.

Fig. 6-15 Cut out two of the four with the pattern flipped.

How-Tos

Sew or serge all seams using 1/4" allowances.

1. On the loop strip, press both long edges 1/4" to the wrong side. Fold the strip again, wrong sides together, matching the folded edges. Edge-stitch along the folds, catching both layers in the stitching.

Serger tip: Decoratively serge-finish the loop strip instead of pressing the edges under. Fold the strip wrong sides together and serge, trimming a scant 1/4" and just catching the folded edge with the left side of the stitching. Use a wide, satin-length, balanced 3- or 3/4-thread stitch and decorative washable thread, such as pearl cotton or cotton crochet thread, in both loopers.

2. Cut the strip into two 6" sections. Pin a loop to the right side of both glove tops on the thumb side, positioning them 1/2" from the lower edge with cut edges aligned. (Fig. 6-16)

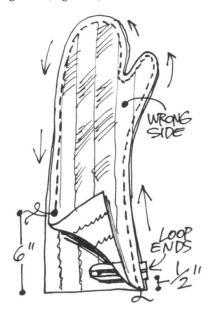

Fig. 6-16 Position the loops before seaming the gloves.

3. With the gloves right sides together, seam the outer edges, beginning at the lower edge below the thumb and ending 6" from the opposite lower edge. If the seam is straight-stitched (instead of serged), finish the seam allowances with zigzagging or another appropriate machine stitch and clip the inside corner.

4. Sew the binding strip, right sides together, to the lower edge of both gloves using a 1/2" seam allowance and easing the binding to the glove.

> **Serger tip:** Serge-finish the bottom edge of the glove to match the loop strip instead of binding it. It is much easier to leave the side of the glove open for 6" and do this step flat. Then finish the side seam in step 5, reinforcing the seamline by straight-stitching through the decorative serging and catching the allowance on the underside. Skip step 6. (Fig. 6-17)

5. With the binding folded out from the glove edge, finish sewing the remaining 6" of the side seams on both gloves, extending the seam through the binding.

6. Fold the binding to the wrong side, pressing the raw edge under 1/2". Straight-stitch on top of the binding near the seamline, catching the folded binding edge on the underside.

Decorative Options

♦ Echo quilt around a pattern in the fabric rather than quilting in parallel rows and/or quilt with a decorative machine stitch instead of straight-stitching.

♦ Cut out the top and bottom sides of the gloves in different colors or coordinating patterns. Bind the edges using a contrasting binding or to match one side.

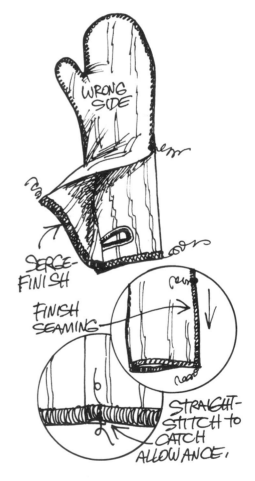

Fig. 6-17 Substitute decorative serging for the binding, if you prefer.

FESTIVE PLACEMATS AND NAPKINS

Give a gift to brighten any meal. Made of shiny lamé, these table toppers are perfect during the holidays or for year-round entertaining. The napkins reverse to a practical cotton/polyester. (Fig. 6-18)

Fig. 6-18 Team lamé and cotton/polyester for a glamorous gift.

Materials Needed

For four placemats and four napkins:

♦ Two yards of 45"-wide washable lamé

♦ Two yards of 45"-wide cotton/polyester fabric

♦ One yard of fusible fleece

♦ Filler cord to match the lamé

Cutting Directions

♦ Fuse the fleece to one yard of the cotton/polyester fabric.

♦ Cut four placemats from the lamé, following the pattern grid. (Fig. 6-19)

♦ Cut four placemats from the fused cotton/polyester.

♦ Cut four 18" by 18" napkin squares from the lamé.

♦ Cut four 18" by 18" napkin squares from the cotton/polyester.

How-Tos

Sew or serge all seams using 1/4" allowances. Use a sharp new needle in the smallest size available. Also use a longer stitch length, and hold the fabric taut while sewing.

1. For each placemat, seam a lamé and a cotton/polyester section right sides together, beginning at the middle of the straight edge, continuing around the curved edge, and leaving an opening for turning.

2. If the seams are straight-stitched, trim them to 1/8" and trim the two corners.

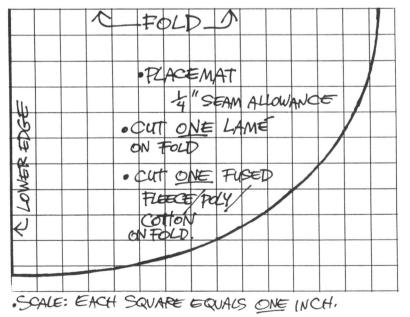

Fig. 6-19 This placemat pattern includes 1/4" seam allowances.

Serger tip: To avoid trimming and turning, decoratively serge-seam the lamé wrong sides together to the cotton/polyester. Use a narrow, satin-length, balanced 3-thread stitch and a matching or contrasting metallic thread in the upper looper. Apply seam sealant at the two corners and clip the threads when dry.

3. Turn the placemats right side out, lightly press them, and pin the edges to keep them aligned. Edge-stitch around the outside of each placemat, closing the openings with the stitching.

4. Quilt the placemats by top-stitching four rows 1-1/4" apart, beginning 1-1/4" from the edge-stitching in one lower corner, following the curve of the top edge to the other corner.

5. Make each napkin by placing one lamé and one cotton/polyester square wrong sides together. Using a narrow zigzag, top-stitch over the filler cord 1/4" from the cut edges on the lamé side, sewing both lengthwise edges first before sewing the crosswise edges. (Fig. 6-20)

6. Carefully trim away the excess allowance close to the stitching. Adjust to a wider, satin-length zigzag and sew over the previous stitching on all four sides.

Serger tips: Finish the napkins using a rolled-edge stitch and decorative thread to match the placemats. First serge the sides on the lengthwise grain and then the sides on the crosswise grain. If threads poke out through the serging, widen the stitch. Or place a strip of water-soluble stabilizer over the cut edges before serging them, then gently tear away the excess stabilizer.

7. Apply seam sealant at the corners and clip the thread ends when dry.

Decorative Options

♦ Use any other decorative fabric (such as a washable tapestry or denim) in place of the lamé.

♦ Quilt the placemat in step 4 using decorative machine stitching.

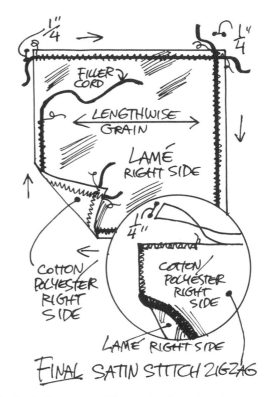

Fig. 6-20 Zigzag over filler cord before trimming away the allowances and zigzagging again.

KNEELING-PAD GARDEN TOTE

Any gardener on your gift list will love this double-handy canvas tote when working in a garden or flower bed, as well as on the patio or veranda. It's a soft kneeling cushion that folds into a carryall for cut flowers and herbs or pruning refuse. (Fig. 6-21)

Fig. 6-21 Layer foam rectangles between heavy canvas so the tote can double as a kneeling pad.

Materials Needed

♦ 1-1/2 yards of 36"-wide heavy cotton, such as canvas or duck (or 3/4 yard of 54"- or 60"-wide fabric)

♦ 3-7/8 yards of 1"-wide cotton webbing

♦ Two 12" by 9" by 1" foam pieces (or one 18" by 12" by 1" piece cut in half lengthwise—it's sold by the foot in fabric stores)

♦ Glue stick for glue-basting

♦ Air-erasable marker

♦ **Optional:** Seam sealant (for the serged-fold self-braid); seam sealant, tear-away stabilizer, paper-backed fusible web, and an *Ultrasuede* remnant large enough to fit in an embroidery hoop (for the identification tag)

Cutting Directions

♦ Cut two 27" by 27" fabric squares.

♦ Place the squares together and fold back two opposite corners 3". Trim, leaving 3/8" seam allowances. (Fig. 6-22)

♦ If you've purchased one large piece of foam, cut it into two 12" by 9" pieces using a serrated-edge knife.

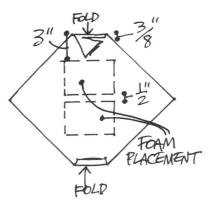

Fig. 6-22 Trim off opposite corners on both tote layers.

How-Tos

1. On the wrong side of one square, lightly mark the foam placement positions, following the above pattern and using an air-erasable marker.

2. Glue-baste the foam pieces to the markings. Place the second fabric square on top of the foam square with wrong sides together. Pin-baste to align the edges and secure the foam.

3. Using a zipper foot, top-stitch around both foam pieces through the two tote layers.

4. Glue-baste around the tote edges, using a 1/4" seam allowance.

5. Cut two 14" pieces of webbing for the handles. Pin the handle ends at each trimmed corner, allowing 1/4" of the webbing to extend past the cut fabric edge. (Fig. 6-23)

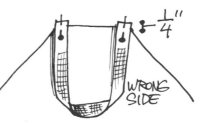

Fig. 6-23 Pin the webbing handles at the trimmed corners on both sides of the tote.

6. Beginning 3/8" from one square (untrimmed) corner, lap the remaining webbing 3/8" over the cut edges of the tote. Seam the webbing to the tote along the overlapped edge, easing around the corners. End 3/8" from the other square corner. Repeat for the opposite sides of the tote, but on this side fold back 1" of the webbing on both ends before seaming it to the tote edges. (Fig. 6-24)

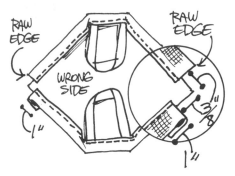

Fig. 6-24 Lap the webbing 3/8" over the edges and top-stitch, beginning and ending 3/8" from the square corners.

7. Wrap the webbing to the other side of the tote, enclosing the cut edges and the handle ends. Fold a miter at each trimmed-edge corner and lap the folded webbing ends over the unfinished ends. Use a pin to tuck in all the cut edges for a neat finish. Top-stitch the unattached edges of the webbing to hold it in place. Top-stitch over the corner miters.

8. Fold the tote in half with the webbing exposed on the outside and the handles at the top.

Decorative Options

♦ Use serged-fold self-braid in place of the webbing for the binding.

1. Press 3/8" to the wrong side around all the tote edges after completing step 4.

2. Tuck the ends of the handles under the 3/8" allowances on the edges of the trimmed corners. (Fig. 6-25)

> **Serger tip:** Instead of using the two 14" pieces of webbing, you may choose to make the handles by decoratively serge-finishing the long edges of 14" by 2" rectangles folded wrong sides together lengthwise. Use a wide, satin-length, balanced 3- or 3/4-thread stitch and heavy decorative thread, such as pearl cotton or pearl rayon, in both loopers.

3. Edge-stitch all of the folds, catching the handle ends. Trim away the allowances close to the stitching. (Fig. 6-26)

4. Using the same thread and settings as described in the previous tip, serge-finish around all of the outer edges, serging slowly over the handle positions.

5. Apply seam sealant to the ends and clip the excess threads when dry.

6. Fold the handles out from the tote and straight-stitch across each end, catching the tote top edge.

♦ Personalize the finished tote by adding an identification tag:

1. Machine-embroider the giftee's name or monogram on a remnant of *Ultrasuede*. Use tear-away stabilizer on the reverse side to keep the fabric from stretching.

2. Cut out a 4" by 2" rectangle with the name or monogram centered in the middle.

3. Cut out a rectangle of paper-backed fusible web just smaller than the *Ultrasuede* rectangle. Center and fuse the web on the wrong side of the rectangle.

4. Remove the paper backing and position and fuse the tag below the handles on one side of the tote. Top-stitch around all four edges to secure it.

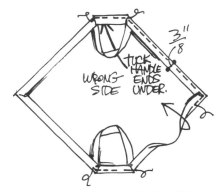

Fig. 6-25 Prepare to apply serged-fold self-braid.

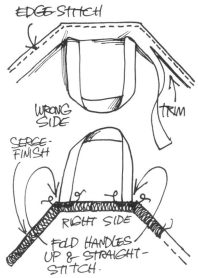

Fig. 6-26 After trimming the excess allowance, serge-finish the outer edges, going on and off the tote at the square corners.

VACUUM ACCESSORY HANG-UP

Help someone special get organized with this practical storage hang-up. It features four pockets designed to hold vacuum cleaner attachments and accessories. (Fig. 6-27)

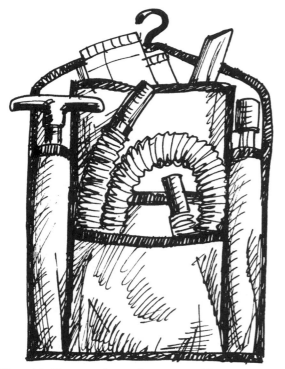

Fig. 6-27 Ripstop nylon and grosgrain ribbon are used to make this vacuum hang-up.

Materials Needed

1-1/4 yards of 60"-wide ripstop nylon

1-1/3 yards of 5/8"-wide grosgrain ribbon

3-3/4 yards of 7/8"-wide grosgrain ribbon

One 16"-wide wire hanger

Cutting Directions

Cut two 16-1/2" by 24" rectangles for the base.

Cut two 4" by 17" rectangles for the side pockets.

Cut one 20" by 24" rectangle for the lower pocket.

♦ Cut one 16" square for the upper pocket.

How-Tos

1. Place the two larger base rectangles wrong sides together and trace around the upper edge of the hanger, adding 3/8" seam allowances. Cut out the curved top. (Fig. 6-28)

Fig. 6-28 Trace the hanger top and add seam allowances before cutting.

2. Press the upper and lower pocket rectangles in half crosswise, wrong sides together. Press 40" of the 7/8"-wide grosgrain ribbon exactly in half lengthwise. Fold the ribbon completely over the pressed pocket edges and top-stitch along the ribbon edge, catching the underlayer of ribbon in the stitching.

3. Cut two 4" sections of grosgrain ribbon and bind one short single-layer end of both side pockets, following the directions in step 2.

4. With the binding on top, position the side pockets on either side of the aligned base pieces, matching the sides and lower edges.

5. Place the unstitched long edges of the side pockets 2-1/2" from the base sides and machine-baste 1/4" from the edges. (Later you'll pleat the excess.)

6. Position the lower pocket on top of the base section, matching the cut edges at the bottom of the bag. Lap the pocket ends 1/2" over the inside edges of the side pockets. Machine-baste the pocket sides 1/4" from the edges. (Fig. 6-29)

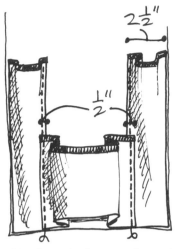

Fig. 6-29 Machine-baste the lower pocket ends over the side pocket edges.

7. Place the lower edges of the upper pocket 3/4" above the top of the lower pocket and lap the sides 1/2" over the inner edges of the side pockets. Machine-baste as in step 6.

8. Insert the hanger between the two base layers and machine-baste around the outside edges, above the side pockets, and across the top, leaving an opening for the hanger hook.

9. Fold one end of the 5/8"-wide grosgrain ribbon 1/2" to the wrong side. Beginning at one upper corner of the upper pocket, top-stitch the ribbon vertically down to the lower edge of the base over the pocket edges. Top-stitch both sides of the ribbon in the same direction. Repeat for the opposite side of the hang-up. (Fig. 6-30)

10. Fold 1/4" pleats in both lower corners of the side pockets, 2" pleats in the lower corners of the lower pocket, and 1" pleats in the lower corners of the upper pocket. Machine-baste the lower pocket edges in place 1/4" from the edge.

11. With 1/2" of the 5/8"-wide grosgrain ribbon folded to the wrong side on both ends, top-stitch it over the lower edge of the upper pocket, beginning and ending at the outer edges of the vertical ribbon. (Fig. 6-31)

12. Press the 7/8"-wide grosgrain ribbon in half lengthwise. Beginning and ending 1/4" from the center top of the base, bind the outer edges, folding under 1/2" of the ribbon on both ends.

Decorative Options

♦ Use black ripstop and several bright colors of grosgrain ribbon for a contemporary color scheme.

♦ Decoratively serge-finish the pocket and outer edges instead of binding them. Do all the machine-basting at slightly less than 1/4". Use a medium- to wide-width, satin-length, balanced 3- or 3/4-thread stitch and decorative thread, such as woolly nylon, in the upper looper. Serge-finish both long edges of a 13" by 5/8" ripstop strip to bind the lower edge of the upper pocket.

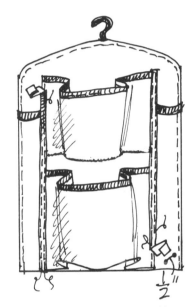

Fig. 6-30 Top-stitch the 5/8" grosgrain ribbon over the pocket edges, turning the ribbon ends under.

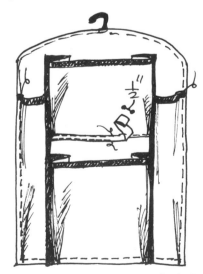

Fig. 6-31 Cover the top pocket's raw edge before binding the hang-up's outer edges.

CHAPTER SEVEN

Gifts with Country Charm

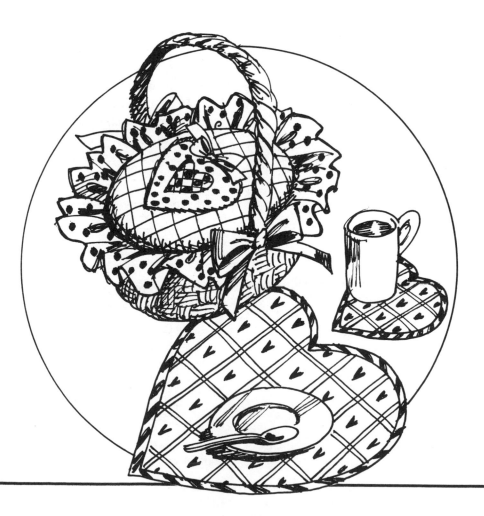

BOW-TIED PAPERWEIGHT

What could be simpler? Sew an octagonal bag, fill it with weighty scented ingredients, and tie the ends together to create a unique paperweight. (Fig. 7-1)

Fig. 7-1 Tie up a fabric paperweight with a pretty satin bow.

Materials Needed

♦ 1/6 yard of tightly woven cotton, such as chintz or gingham

♦ 1/2 yard of 1-1/2"-wide double-faced satin ribbon

♦ Approximately one cup of lentils or rice

♦ Scented potpourri oil, found in craft stores

Cutting Directions

♦ Cut two fabric octagons following the pattern grid. (Fig. 7-2)

♦ Cut the ribbon into two 9" pieces.

How-Tos

Sew or serge all seams using 1/4" allowances.

1. Fold the ribbon pieces wrong sides together and match the cut edges of each to the opposite short ends of one octagon's right side.

> **Serger tip:** Instead of using a ribbon, cut two 1-3/4" by 18" strips of matching or coordinating fabric. With wrong sides together, decoratively serge the long edges using a rolled-edge stitch, decorative thread in the upper looper, and monofilament nylon thread in the lower looper. Cut the strip into two 9"-long strips and begin step 1.

2. Place the octagons right sides together and sew around the outside edges, being careful not to catch the loose ends of the ribbon and leaving an opening for turning and stuffing on one long edge.

3. Turn the bag right side out and press carefully. Stuff it with rice or lentils that you've scented, following the manufacturer's instructions on the potpourri oil.

4. Hand-sew the opening closed. Top-stitch 1/4" from the edge around the entire paperweight, moving the "stuffing" aside as you sew.

5. Shake the stuffing toward the center. Knot the ribbons at the top of the paperweight to form a bow.

Decorative Options

♦ Top-stitch or glue decorative trim on the outside edges of the bag.

♦ Decoratively serge-finish the edges with the fabric wrong sides together. Position the ribbon ties following the directions in step 1. Serge-finish the edges using a medium- to wide-width, satin-length, balanced 3-thread stitch with decorative thread in both loopers. Serge on and off each edge, catching the ribbon ends in the serging. On one long edge, leave an opening to insert the stuffing. After stuffing, serge-finish the opening to close, overlapping the previous stitching 1/2" on both sides. Apply seam sealant at the corners, allow it to dry, and clip thread ends.

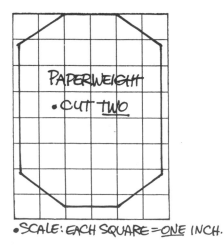

• SCALE: EACH SQUARE = ONE INCH.

Fig. 7-2 The paperweight pattern includes 1/4" seam allowances.

HEART-SHAPED PLACEMATS AND COASTERS

Add country charm to someone's table or entertaining by giving them heart-shaped placemats and coasters. Use a quilted fabric, such as gingham, calico, or even a Christmas plaid, to add to the rustic spirit. (Fig. 7-3)

Fig. 7-3 Send stacks of warm wishes along with these fanciful table toppers.

Materials Needed

For six placemats:
♦ 2-1/3 yards of 45"-wide quilted cotton fabric (or 1-3/4 yards of 60"-wide fabric)

♦ Ten yards of wide matching or coordinating bias tape

For seven coasters:
♦ 1/3 yard of 45"-wide quilted cotton fabric (or 1/3 yard of 60"-wide fabric for ten coasters)

♦ 4 yards of wide matching or coordinating bias tape (or 5-5/8 yards for ten coasters)

Cutting Directions

For the placemats:
♦ Cut 12 hearts using pattern grid A. (Grids C and D are used in later projects.) (Fig. 7-4)

For the coasters:
♦ Cut 14 hearts from 45"-wide fabric (or 20 hearts from 60"-wide fabric) using pattern grid B.

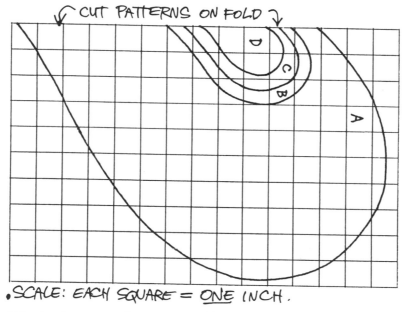

Fig. 7-4 Use this pattern grid for the placemats and coasters, as well as for later projects.

How-Tos

Follow the same directions for both the placemats and the coasters.

1. Pin two hearts wrong sides together and machine-baste around the cut edges.

2. Beginning at the lower point, straight-stitch the opened bias tape, right sides together, to the heart edges. Stitch along the outer press-line of the tape, easing it around the curves and pivoting at the upper center point. To finish the binding, fold the beginning of the tape over the heart's cut edge and wrap the finishing end to the wrong side over the top. (Fig. 7-5)

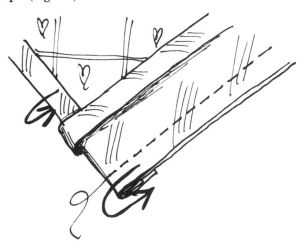

Fig. 7-5 At the bottom point, wrap the beginning binding around the edge before folding the opened end of the tape over it.

> **Serger tip:** Instead of binding the edge, decoratively serge-finish it using a medium- to wide-width, short, balanced 3-thread stitch and heavy washable thread, such as buttonhole twist, #8 pearl cotton, or cotton crochet thread, in both loopers. Beginning and ending at the bottom point, serge around the edges, pulling the fabric straight as you serge around the upper center point. Dab the ends with seam sealant, allow them to dry, and clip the excess threads. To negotiate the curved edges more easily, narrow the stitch and serge slowly, pulling the fabric straight in front of the presser foot.

3. Wrap the bias tape tightly to the wrong side and steam press it into position, folding the tape to miter it at the upper center point. Stitch-in-the-ditch from the right side to secure the tape edge on the underside.

4. For added appeal, stack the coasters or placemats and tie them together with decorative ribbon.

Decorative Options

♦ Quilt any fabric using 2-1/3 yards of 45"-wide (or 1-3/4 yards of 60"-wide) cotton fabric and 7/8 yard of fleece for the placemats and 1/3 yard of 45"-wide (or 1/3 yard of 60"-wide) cotton fabric and 1/6 yard of fleece for the coasters. Pin the fleece securely between two layers of the fabric and quilt from the right side, using intersecting diagonal rows of stitching or any other desired stitching pattern.

♦ Decoratively serge-finish the placemats or coasters instead of binding them, following the directions after step 2.

SCENTED HOT PAD

Give a gift that protects the table and adds a sweet scent at the same time. Potpourri hidden under the decorative heart releases its fragrance as hot dishes are placed on top of it. (Fig. 7-6)

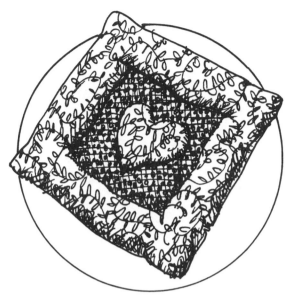

Fig. 7-6 The finished hot pad is approximately 10" square.

Materials Needed

♦ 1/3 yard of tightly woven cotton fabric

♦ One 7"-square remnant of contrasting fabric

♦ 1/3 yard of heavy batting

♦ One 12" square of *Teflon*-coated fabric

♦ One 6" square of tear-away stabilizer

♦ Simmering potpourri, found in craft, fabric, and general merchandise stores

Cutting Directions

From the cotton fabric:

♦ Cut one heart following pattern grid B in Fig. 7-4.

♦ Cut two 11" squares.

From the contrasting fabric:

♦ Cut one 6-1/2" square.

From the batting:

♦ Cut two 11" squares.

From the *Teflon*-coated fabric:

♦ Cut one 11" square.

How-Tos

Sew or serge all seams using 1/4" allowances.

1. Center the heart on the contrasting 6-1/2" square. With tear-away stabilizer on the wrong side and a

small amount of potpourri under the heart, appliqué the heart to the square. Carefully tear away the stabilizer.

2. Center the appliquéd square on the right side of one of the larger squares. Appliqué the contrasting square's edges over the larger square.

> **Serger tip:** To serge-appliqué for both of the previous steps, adjust for a rolled edge, using a matching or coordinating color thread (either serger weight or all-purpose) in the upper looper. (Do not use woolly nylon thread for this application because of its low melting point.) When serging around the heart, begin and end at the lower point, pulling the fabric straight at the upper center point. Top-stitch the serge-finished heart and square over the underlayer, close to the rolled edge.

3. Stack from the bottom: one batting square, the *Teflon*-coated square (silver side up), the second batting square, the appliquéd square (right side up), and the plain fabric square (wrong side up). Straight-stitch around the outer edges, leaving an opening on one side for turning. (Fig. 7-7)

4. Trim the corners and turn the pad right side out. Hand-sew the opening closed.

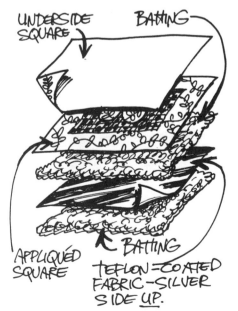

Fig. 7-7 Layer the components before seaming the outer edges.

Serger tip: To decoratively finish the hot pad, place the fabric squares wrong sides together, sandwiching the batting squares with the *Teflon*-coated square (silver side up) between them. Serge-finish the edges through all layers using a wide, satin-length, balanced 3-thread stitch and a heavy washable thread, such as pearl cotton or crochet thread, in both loopers.

5. Quilt the hot pad by top-stitching through all layers around the heart and the edge of the appliquéd square, next to the appliqué stitching.

Decorative Options

♦ Make the pad reversible by using a different color for the two 11" by 11" squares and two back-to-back squares of *Teflon*-coated fabric.

♦ Decoratively serge-finish the appliqué and pad edges, following the directions after steps 2 and 4.

RUFFLED NAPKINS AND NAPKIN RINGS

Color-coordinate the ruffles on these delightful napkins and rings to complement anyone's decor. Use a solid color for the napkins, and use calico, gingham, or chintz for the ruffles. (Fig. 7-8)

Fig. 7-8 Give place settings a country feeling with ruffles, hearts, and a winsome fabric.

Materials Needed

♦ 7/8 yard of 45"-wide cotton fabric for six napkins (60"-wide fabric makes eight)

♦ One yard of a contrasting print fabric

♦ 1/3 yard of paper-backed fusible web

♦ Seam sealant

♦ Glue gun and glue or all-purpose craft glue

Cutting Directions

♦ Cut six (or eight) 15" napkin squares from the cotton fabric.

♦ Fuse the web to the wrong side of a portion of the contrasting fabric.

♦ Cut one fused heart for each napkin from grid C in Fig. 7-4.

♦ Cut one 3" by 10" fused strip for every two napkin rings.

♦ Cut one 2" by 10" bias strip from unfused contrasting fabric for each napkin ring.

♦ Cut the remaining unfused contrasting fabric into 1-1/2"-wide bias strips for the napkin ruffles. Piece, using 1/4" seam allowances, to make strips approximately 75" long for each napkin.

How-Tos

1. Finish all the napkin edges with 1/8"-wide double hems.

> **Serger tip:** Serge-hem the napkins using a satin-length rolled-edge stitch and serger-weight or all-purpose thread in the upper looper. Lettuce the ruffle edges in steps 3 and 8 using the same stitch and stretching as you serge. Adjust the differential feed, if available, to the lowest setting to assist with the lettucing.

2. Remove the paper backing from the fused hearts. Place the bottom of one heart 3-1/2" from one corner of each napkin and fuse. Appliqué around the heart edges. (Fig. 7-9)

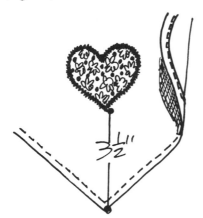

Fig. 7-9 Fuse and appliqué the hearts on one corner of each napkin.

3. Lettuce all four edges of the napkin ruffle strips by zigzagging along the edge (with the right side of the stitch going off the fabric) using a medium-width, short-length stitch and stretching as you sew. Dab seam sealant at each corner and trim the excess threads when dry.

4. Gather the ruffle strips by machine-basting lengthwise down the center of each. Gather each strip to fit a napkin with the center of the ruffle next to the hemmed edge and easing extra fabric into the corners. Begin and end at the corner opposite the appliquéd corner, overlapping the ends. (Fig. 7-10)

5. Top-stitch the ruffles to the napkin over the center gathering stitches.

6. Begin the napkin rings by removing the paper backing from the fused strips. Fold the strips in thirds lengthwise and fuse well.

7. Cut each strip into two 5" lengths. Overlap the ends 1/2" and glue them securely to form the rings.

8. Lettuce the edges of the bias strips for the napkin rings, following the directions in step 3. Machine-gather down the lengthwise center of each to make the napkin ring ruffles.

9. Glue one ruffle around the outside of each ring, overlapping the ends 1/2" to finish.

Decorative Options

♦ Instead of traditional country-inspired colors and prints, use a patriotic red, white, and blue color scheme–perhaps for a Fourth of July hostess gift?

♦ Wrap a narrow ribbon or piece of twine around the center of the napkin rings and tie the ends into a bow. Use a drop of glue under the knot to hold it in place.

Fig. 7-10 Overlap the napkin ruffle ends at the corner opposite the appliqué.

HEARTS GALORE

Whip up a batch of hearts for a multitude of gifts. Stack various sizes for an ornament or pincushion. Arrange them on a ring for a wall hanging or centerpiece. (Fig. 7-11)

Fig. 7-11 Put your pinking shears to work making a variety of heart-shaped gifts.

Materials Needed

For the stacked hearts:
◆ Two 6" squares of Fabric 1

   Two 4-1/2" squares of Fabric 2

◆ Two 4" squares of Fabric 3

   Polyester fiberfill

   One yard of 1/8"-wide ribbon

   One small ribbon rose

   For the ring of hearts:
   1/6 yard of tightly woven fabric

◆ One 8" metal ring

   Polyester fiberfill

   Three yards of 1/8"-wide ribbon

   Optional: Glue gun and glue or all-purpose craft glue

Cutting Directions

For the stacked hearts:
◆ Cut two hearts from Fabric 1 using grid B (see Fig. 7-4).

◆ Cut two hearts from Fabric 2 using grid C.

◆ Cut two hearts from Fabric 3 using grid D.

For the ring of hearts:
◆ Cut 16 hearts using grid D (again see Fig. 7-4).

How-Tos

Sew using 1/4" seam allowances.

1. Make all of the hearts by placing two layers wrong sides together and straight-stitching approximately two-thirds of the way around, beginning at the bottom point. Stuff the heart with fiberfill and continue stitching around the remaining edge.

2. Pink the raw edges, barely trimming the fabric. Readjust the fiberfill so it is evenly distributed inside the heart. (Fig. 7-12)

Fig. 7-12 Trim off as little fabric as possible when pinking the raw edges.

For the stacked hearts:

1. Stack the three hearts, centering the medium-sized one over the largest one, with the smallest on top. Hand-sew the hearts together straight through the centers of all three.

2. Cut the ribbon into three 5" pieces. Loop them at the center of the smallest heart with the tails hanging down. Hand-sew the ribbon centers to the heart with the rose on top. (Fig. 7-13)

3. Use the remaining ribbon for a loop at the top if you are making a hanging ornament. Hand-sew the ribbon ends to the upper center point on the back of the largest heart.

Fig. 7-13 Embellish the stacked hearts with ribbon and a rose.

For the ring of hearts:

1. Place the eight hearts over the ring with the lower points toward the center. Hand-sew the hearts together at their side edges and to the ring directly behind where they are each joined.

2. Without cutting the ribbon, tie eight bows evenly along it, forming a complete circle. Hand-sew or glue one bow over each point at which the hearts are connected.

Decorative Options

♦ Top-stitch or glue narrow lace or eyelet with one straight edge on top of the outer heart edges. (Fig. 7-14)

Fig. 7-14 Glue or top-stitch lace or eyelet over the pinked edges, turning under and lapping the end.

♦ Stuff the hearts with potpourri for a sweet-smelling gift—the individual hearts make great sachets, too.

♦ Make a small lapel-pin heart out of denim; hand-sew or glue a bow on the front and a barpin on the back.

EMBROIDERY-HOOP WALL HANGING

Create the feeling of a bygone era using a simple embroidery hoop and a distinctive floral print. Trapunto adds a lifelike quality to the flowers inside the hoop. (Fig. 7-15)

Fig. 7-15 Trapunto accentuates the floral shapes on this ruffled wall hanging.

Materials Needed

♦ 1/2 yard of 45"-wide fabric with a large, definite floral print

♦ 1/3 yard of lightweight backing fabric, such as muslin or batiste

♦ 7/8 yard of 1-1/2"-wide ruffled eyelet trim with one scalloped edge

♦ 1/2 yard of 7/8"-wide ribbon

♦ One 8" wooden embroidery hoop

♦ Polyester fiberfill

♦ Filler cord

Cutting Directions

♦ Cut one 10-1/2" floral fabric circle.

♦ Cut one 3-1/2" by 56" floral fabric strip for the ruffle, piecing if necessary.

♦ Cut one 10-1/2" circle from the backing fabric.

How-Tos

Sew or serge all seams using 1/4" allowances.

1. With the wrong sides of the two fabric circles together, machine-baste around the outer edge.

2. From the right side of the circle, straight-stitch around the floral motifs. From the back side, slit the backing fabric in the center of each motif. Lightly stuff each with fiberfill and hand-sew the openings closed (or fuse them closed with mending tape). (Fig. 7-16)

Fig. 7-16 Create the trapunto detailing by slitting the backing fabric, stuffing each shape with fiberfill, and hand-sewing each closed.

3. Machine-baste the eyelet, right sides together, to the outer edge of the fabric circle, turning the beginning end of the strip to the wrong side and lapping the other end 1/2" to finish.

4. Sew the ruffle strip into a circle with right sides together. Using a narrow zigzag, top-stitch over the filler cord 1/4" from one long edge.

5. Trim away the allowance close to the stitching. Adjust for a wider, satin-length zigzag and sew over the previous stitching.

Serger tip: Serge-finish one long edge of the ruffle strip using a rolled edge instead of zig-zagging over cording.

6. Machine-gather the unfinished long edge of the strip to fit the outside of the circle. Place the ruffle right sides together with the outer edge of the fabric circle, sandwiching the eyelet trim between.

7. Sew the ruffle and eyelet to the outer edge of the circle. Center the ruffled circle in the hoop with the hoop clamp at the top, pulling the fabric taut in the hoop and spreading the ruffles evenly.

8. Tie the ribbon into a bow and hand-sew it at the top of the hoop, covering the clamp.

Decorative Options

♦ Choose a solid-color fabric and appliqué flowers inside the hoop without using a backing fabric. Use the same trapunto method to raise the appliqués by slitting the solid-color fabric on the underside.

♦ Machine- or hand-embroider a design inside the hoop instead of using trapunto.

FOLD-UP PILLOW COMFORTER

This versatile gift serves two purposes—it's both a snuggly cocoon-shaped comforter and an attractive throw pillow. The foot-warmer pocket at the comforter bottom is the secret, holding the rest of the comforter when it's folded to form the pillow. (Fig. 7-17)

Fig. 7-17 They'll be both warm and comfortable when you give this dual-duty gift.

Materials Needed

♦ 3-2/3 yards of 45"-wide woven cotton/polyester fabric

♦ 2-1/4 yards of 45"-wide polyester batting (or one twin-sheet-size piece)

Cutting Directions

♦ Cut two 45" by 54" fabric rectangles for the comforter.

♦ Cut one 20" by 40" fabric rectangle for the pocket.

♦ Cut one 45" by 54" batting rectangle for the comforter.

♦ Cut one 20" batting square for the pocket.

How-Tos

Sew or serge all seams using 1/4" allowances.

1. Fold the pocket rectangle crosswise with wrong sides together and sandwich the batting square in the middle. Top-stitch 1/4" from the fold. Using a long narrow zigzag stitch, machine-baste the remaining cut edges together.

2. With both right side up, center the pocket on one fabric rectangle, matching the lower cut edges. Machine-baste the pocket to the rectangle close to the pocket's cut edges–this will be the comforter front. (Fig. 7-18)

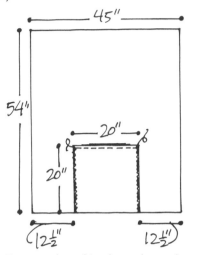

Fig. 7-18 Center and machine-baste the pocket on the lower edge of the comforter front.

3. Place the comforter rectangles right sides together with the batting rectangle underneath and the pocket sandwiched in between. Sew around the outer edges, leaving an opening for turning.

4. Trim the corners and turn the comforter right side out. Hand-sew the opening closed. Top-stitch around the comforter 1/4" from the edges.

5. Mark two lengthwise lines, each 12" from either side of the comforter directly above the pocket edges. Top-stitch along the lines through all layers. (Fig. 7-19)

6. Fold the comforter front, right sides together, exactly on the stitched lines. From the back of the comforter, top-stitch through all layers 1/4" from the folds, catching the pocket edges in the stitching.

7. To form the pillow, fold the lengthwise edges to the back side along the stitching lines. Turn the pocket wrong side out, enclosing the lower third of the comforter. Fold the remaining comforter in half toward the pocket and fold once again, inserting it inside the pocket. (Fig. 7-20)

Decorative Options

♦ Appliqué a design on both sides of the pocket before beginning step 1. One side will show on the pillow and the other will be featured on the foot-warmer pocket when the comforter is folded out.

♦ For a quilted look, use a fabric you have pieced from scraps or select a fabric that is printed to replicate quilting.

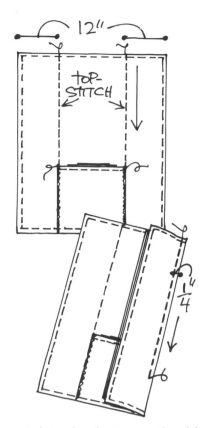

Fig. 7-19 Top-stitch two lengthwise rows, then fold along the stitching and top-stitch again.

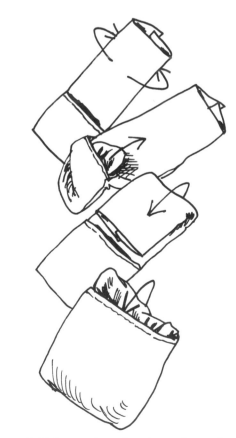

Fig. 7-20 Fold the comforter into the pocket to shape the pillow.

TIE-ON SEAT PADS

Furnish an extra measure of country charm to anyone who loves this nostalgic look. These comfortable reversible cushions tie on to most straight-back chairs. (Fig. 7-21)

Fig. 7-21 Here's a practical gift someone will love to use—colorful cushions for the dining room or breakfast nook.

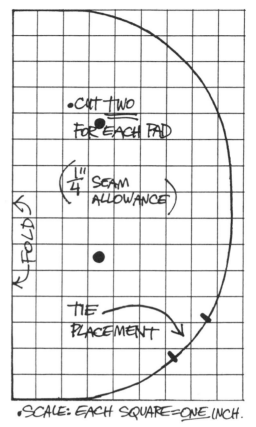

Fig. 7-22 Cut two pad shapes for each cushion.

Materials Needed

♦ 2-1/4 yards 45"-wide fabric for four seat pads

♦ Polyester fiberfill

Cutting Directions

♦ Cut two pad shapes for each chair, following the pattern grid. (Fig. 7-22)

♦ Cut eight 4-1/2" by 45" strips for the ties.

♦ Cut six 6" by 45" strips for the ruffles.

How-Tos

Sew or serge all seams using 1/4" allowances.

1. Fold the tie strips in half lengthwise, right sides together, and seam the long edges. Cut each strip into two equal lengths. Sew a slanted seam across one end of every piece.

> **Serger tip:** Serge-finish the ties by folding the strips wrong sides together and seaming the long edge and slanted ends with a short rolled-edge stitch.

2. Turn the ties right side out and press carefully. With the cut edges matching, pin two ties at each placement mark on the right sides of four pad shapes. **Note:** If you have access to the gift recipient's chairs, place a pad piece on one to mark the best tie placement for that chair. Duplicate the markings for three more pads.

3. Piece the ruffle strips to form four lengths, approximately 66" long. Sew each into a circle.

4. Fold the circles in half lengthwise, wrong sides together, and machine-baste the cut edges together. Gather and pin the ruffles, right sides together, around the outer edges of the same four pad shapes, matching the cut edges and sandwiching the tie ends in between. Machine-baste the edges through all layers.

Serger tip: After folding the ruffle strip wrong sides together, decoratively serge-finish the folded edge using a short rolled-edge stitch. Serge-gather the opposite long edge by using a long, wide, balanced 3-thread stitch and adjusting the differential feed to its lowest setting. For more gathering, you may want to tighten the needle tension as well.

5. Place one of the remaining pad shapes, right sides together, on each of the previous four, sandwiching the ruffle and ties in between. Sew around the pad edges, leaving an opening at the back for turning and making sure not to catch the ruffle or ties in the stitching.

6. Turn the pads right side out and press carefully. Stuff each with fiberfill, making certain to distribute it evenly.

7. Hand-sew the opening closed on each pad. At the placement dots, hand-sew through all layers several times, tufting the cushions. (Fig. 7-23)

Decorative Options

♦ For a contrasting ruffle and ties, purchase one yard of primary fabric and 1-1/3 yards of a second fabric for four seat pads.

♦ Make a set of placemats and napkins to coordinate with the seat pads for a complete effect.

Fig. 7-23 Tuft each cushion at the four places indicated on the pattern.

LINED AND LIDDED COUNTRY BASKET

Make an enchanting round basket anyone will appreciate. It's fully lined and covered with a puffed and appliquéd lid. Choose a fabric to complement any decor or taste. (Fig. 7-24)

Fig. 7-24 Turn a simple basket into a valued helper. The liner and lid keep the contents safe and secure.

Materials Needed

♦ Select a round basket with a handle, 10" in diameter or less. Then determine the yardage needed and cutting requirements by taking four measurements:

Measurement A—Beginning at the top edge on one side of the basket, measure down inside the basket, across the bottom, and up the opposite side to the top. Add 1" to this length. (Fig. 7-25)

Measurement B—Measure the circumference of the basket top.

Measurement C—Measure the diameter of the basket top.

Measurement D—Measure the diameter of the inside bottom of the basket.

♦ 45"-wide or wider print fabric the length of measurement A plus measurement C plus 5"

45"-wide fusible fleece equal to measurement C plus 1"

One 5"-square remnant of a contrasting fabric for the larger heart

♦ One 3"-square remnant of a different contrasting fabric for the smaller heart

Paper-backed fusible web three times measurement C plus 1"

♦ 1/2 yard of 1/4"-wide ribbon

Two circles of heavy cardboard—one the diameter of measurement C and one the diameter of measurement D

Filler cord

♦ Glue gun and glue

Cutting Directions

From the print fabric:
Cut one basket liner circle with a diameter equal to measurement A.

Cut one ruffle strip 4"-wide by twice measurement B, piecing if necessary.

♦ Cut two circles with a diameter equal to measurement C plus 1" for the lid.

♦ Cut one circle with a diameter equal to measurement D plus 1" for the basket bottom.

♦ Cut two 2-1/2" by 24" strips for the ties.

From the two contrasting fabrics:
♦ Fuse paper-backed web to the wrong side of both remnants.

♦ Cut one heart from the 5"-square fused fabric, following grid C (see Fig. 7-4).

♦ Cut one heart from the 3"-square fused fabric, following grid D.

From the fleece:
♦ Cut two circles with a diameter equal to measurement C for the basket lid.

♦ Cut one circle with a diameter equal to measurement C plus 1" for the basket lid.

♦ Cut one circle with a diameter equal to measurement D plus 1" for the basket bottom.

From the paper-backed fusible web:
♦ Cut two circles with a diameter equal to measurement C plus 1" for the basket lid.

♦ Cut one circle with a diameter equal to measurement D plus 1" for the basket bottom.

How-Tos

Sew or serge all seams using 1/4" allowances.

1. Sew the ruffle strip into a circle with right sides together. Fold the circle lengthwise with wrong sides together and gather the aligned cut edges to fit the edge of the basket liner.

2. Sew the ruffle to the liner with right sides together.

3. Sew over the filler cord on the seam allowance, using a long wide zigzag stitch and being careful not to stitch through the cord. Put the lining in the basket and draw up the filler cord to fit the top edge. Mark the tie placement even with the basket handles on the liner wrong side.

4. Press both tie strips in half lengthwise, wrong sides together. Fold 3/8" to the wrong side on each end. Then press the lengthwise cut edges in to meet the fold and press again. Edge-stitch next to the open folded edges and ends.

5. Mark the halfway point of each tie and sew it to the marked tie placements on the wrong side of the basket lining. (Fig. 7-26)

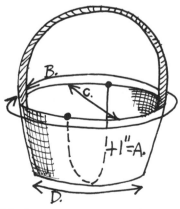

Fig. 7-25 Take four measurements to determine the necessary fabric and cutting measurements to accurately complete the project.

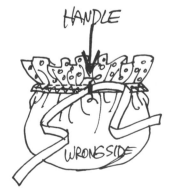

Fig. 7-26 Sew the center of the ties to the handle positions on the wrong side of the liner.

6. Place the lining in the basket wrong side down with the ruffle seamline wrapped slightly over the upper edge. Glue the liner in place along the seamline.

7. Construct the basket bottom by fusing the fleece to the wrong side of the fabric. Then fuse the paper-backed web to the back of the fused fleece circle. Remove the paper backing.

8. From the right side of the basket bottom, zigzag over filler cord close to the cut edges, following the procedure in step 3. Center the measurement-D cardboard circle on the wrong side of the fused circles. Pull up the filler cord to gather the edge snuggly and tie it securely. Fuse the web to the cardboard from the right side.

9. Insert the basket bottom, right side up, into the basket and glue it in place.

10. Fuse the smaller fleece lid circle to the top of the measurement-C cardboard circle to begin the lid. Then fuse the larger fleece circle to the wrong side of one fabric circle for the lid top and the smaller fleece circle to the other fabric circle for the lid underside. (Fig. 7-27)

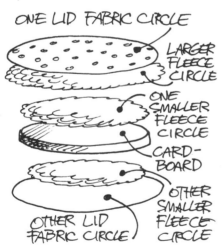

Fig. 7-27 Fuse the lid components before appliquéing the top and joining the three sections with fusible web.

11. Remove the backing on the hearts and center the larger one on the right side of the lid top circle. Fuse it in place. Center the smaller heart over the other one and fuse it. Appliqué the outer edges of both hearts to the fabric and fleece.

12. Fuse the paper-backed web over the exposed sides of the two larger fleece circles. Before removing the paper backing on the lid underside, press the outer fabric edges over the fleece, molding the allowance evenly. Then remove the paper backing and fuse the allowance to the underside, being careful not to touch the web with the iron. (Fig. 7-28)

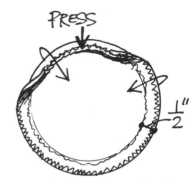

Fig. 7-28 On the lid underside, wrap the edges evenly to the wrong side.

13. Zigzag over filler cord on the right side of the appliquéd circle, following the directions in step 3. Center the cardboard circle, fleece side down, on the wrong side of the appliquéd circle. Pull up the filler cord to gather the edges evenly and knot securely. Fuse from the right side.

14. With wrong sides together, place the upper lid and the underside together and fuse from the underside. Hand-sew to secure the edges.

15. Tie the ribbon into a bow and glue or hand-sew it at the upper center point of the heart.

Decorative Options

♦ Cut the smaller heart of solid-color fabric with decorative stitching, machine-embroidery, or lettering on it. Consider using a short saying or the giftee's name.

♦ Decoratively serge-finish both heart edges using a satin-length rolled-edge stitch. Serge on and off at the bottom point and pull the upper center point out straight in front of the machine as you serge over it. Top-stitch the hearts to the basket top, with the smaller one centered on top.

CHAPTER EIGHT
Gifts for the Bath and Boudoir

SOAP-SAVER WASHCLOTHS

These little terry scrubbers have a pocket to hold small bars of soap and soap scraps—a useful and practical gift. They hang to dry from the loop at the top. (Fig. 8-1)

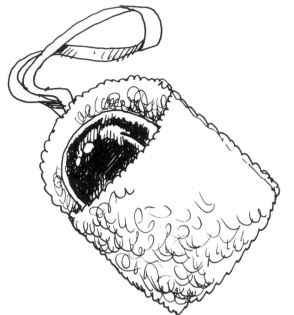

Fig. 8-1 With these soap savers, they can use every bar down to the last bubble.

Materials Needed

♦ 1/6 yard of terry cloth (make three from 45"-wide fabric or four from 60"-wide fabric)

♦ 9" of 1/4"-wide polyester twill tape

Cutting Directions

Cut one 15" by 5" terry cloth rectangle.

How-Tos

Sew or serge all seams using 1/4" allowances.

1. On one short end of the rectangle, fold a 1/2" double hem to the wrong side and top-stitch along the hem edge.

2. Finish the other short end by zigzagging or serging the edge. Fold back 5" of this end right sides together. Round the corners and trim the folded edge. (Fig. 8-2)

3. Pin the ends of the twill tape to the center of the curved edges between the two layers of fabric, matching the cut edges.

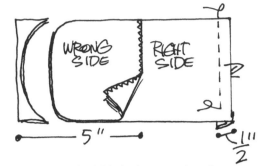

Fig. 8-2 Trim the folded edge, rounding the corners.

4. Fold back 4" of the hemmed end, positioning it beneath the other end. Pull the hem edges slightly out from the seam allowances on both sides so the top of the pocket will be a little narrower. Sew around the three raw-edge sides, being careful to catch only the ends of the tape in the stitching. Zigzag-finish the seam allowances if the seam was straight-stitched. (Fig. 8-3)

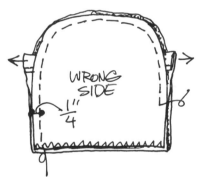

Fig. 8-3 Pull the hem edges out slightly as you seam the pocket.

5. Turn the cloth right side out through the opening and then turn the pocket right side out.

Decorative Options

♦ To add a feminine touch and more scrubbing power, top-stitch 1"-wide strips of gathered nylon net to the right side of the hemmed end after completing step 3.

♦ Monogram or machine-embroider just below the hem on the right side.

SLEEP-COMFORT BODY PILLOW

Give a gift of comfort that absorbs body weight more evenly. It's especially helpful for someone who has back problems or is pregnant and can also double as a read-in-bed backrest. (Fig. 8-4)

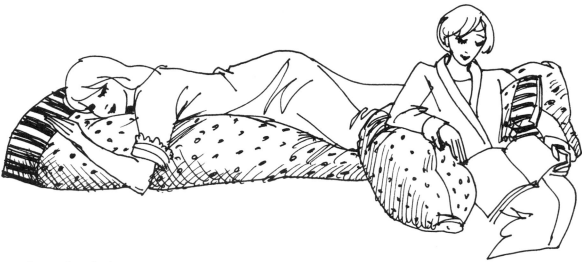

Fig. 8-4 Make a 5'-long body pillow with its own special pillowcase.

Materials Needed

♦ 1-1/4 yards of 60"-wide woven cotton/polyester fabric for the pillow

♦ Approximately 6 lbs. (96 oz.) of polyester fiberfill

♦ 1-1/3 yards of 60"-wide fashion fabric for the pillowcase

♦ 1/3 yard of 54"-wide or wider contrasting fabric for the pillowcase band

Cutting Directions

♦ Cut the pillow and pillowcase yardage to the exact lengths given.

♦ Cut one 12" by 48" rectangle from the contrasting band fabric.

How-Tos

Sew or serge all seams using 1/4" allowances. If the pillowcase seams are straight-stitched, zigzag-finish the allowances.

1. Fold the pillow fabric in half with the 60" width running lengthwise. Sew both ends and the long raw edges, leaving an opening for turning and stuffing. As you sew, round the corners slightly to avoid having pointed corners.

2. Turn the pillow right side out and press it. Stuff the fiberfill inside evenly so the pillow is firm but still flexible enough for comfort. Edge-stitch the opening closed.

3. On one long edge of the contrasting band rectangle, press 1/4" to the wrong side. With right sides together, sew the opposite edge to one shorter side of the pillowcase fabric for the top band. Press the seam allowances toward the band.

4. Fold the pillowcase right sides together lengthwise, matching the raw edges and the seamlines. Sew the side and bottom edges, folding out the pressed allowance on the band.

5. Fold the band to the wrong side, just covering the seamline. From the right side, stitch-in-the-ditch to secure, making sure to catch the folded edge underneath. (Fig. 8-5)

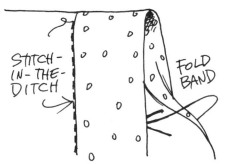

Fig. 8-5 Finish the pillowcase by folding the band edge to the inside and securing it with the stitch-in-the-ditch.

Decorative Options

♦ Sew several pillowcases with a variety of ornamental touches. Insert piping or lace in the seam between the band and the case. Add a monogram or machine embroidery. Scallop the band edge using a reverse blindhem stitch or a shell stitch. (Fig. 8-6)

♦ Decoratively serge all of the pillowcase seams using a satin-length, balanced 3-thread stitch and exposing the allowances on the outside.

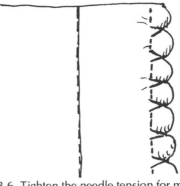

Fig. 8-6 Tighten the needle tension for more scalloping.

LACY LIGHT-SWITCH COVER

For the woman who has "everything," this feminine switch-plate cover adds an elegant touch to her bathroom, bedroom, or dressing area. No more plain plastic for her! (Fig. 8-7)

Fig. 8-7 Cover and decorate a light switch to dress up her bathroom or boudoir.

Materials Needed

♦ One switch plate (available at hardware stores)

♦ One piece of fabric, such as taffeta or satin, 1" larger than the length and width of the switch plate

♦ One piece of lightweight batting, 1/2" larger than the length and width of the switch plate

♦ 1-1/3 yards of 1"-wide ruffled lace with one scalloped edge

♦ Air-erasable marker

♦ Glue gun and glue

Cutting Directions

♦ Center the switch plate on the batting and use a marking pen to draw the switch opening(s) and trace around the plate's outer edges. Cut the batting on the traced lines and trim out the switch opening(s).

♦ Center the switch plate on the right side of the fabric and draw the seamline by lightly tracing around the edges using the air-erasable marker. Mark the switch opening(s) and screw holes. (If the holes are closed, punch them open using one of the screws.) Slit the switch opening(s), cutting diagonal slits to the corners. (Fig. 8-8)

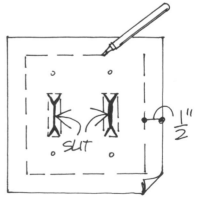

Fig. 8-8 Mark the seamline, switch opening(s), and screw holes. Then slit the fabric at the switch opening(s).

How-Tos

1. Remove the gathering stitches from 2/3 yard of the lace and press it flat. With the scalloped edge toward the center, top-stitch the straight edge of the lace right side up over the right side of the fabric along the bottom seamline of the fabric rectangle. Repeat for the top of the rectangle and then both sides.

2. Fold 1/2" to the wrong side on one end of the ruffled lace. Beginning at a lower corner, sew the ruffled lace, right sides together, to the rectangle with the straight edge over the flat straight lace edges. Ease the gathered lace around the corners and lap the end 1/2" over the beginning fold. (Fig. 8-9)

3. Glue the batting to the switch plate. Place the wrong side of the fabric rectangle over the batting and wrap the edges of the switch opening(s) and sides to the back of the switch plate. Glue, stretching firmly.

Fig. 8-9 Sew on all of the lace before gluing the fabric to the switch plate.

Decorative Options

♦ Purchase 3/4 yard of pearl beading and glue it around the outer edge of the switch plate on top of the ruffled lace seamline.

♦ Use different fabric and trim to complement any decor. Consider ruffled eyelet and calico, or make a ruffle to match a decorator print cover.

EXQUISITE EMBELLISHED TOWELS

They'll love your personal touch on a set of soft and fluffy towels. Choose from our easy options or use your creativity. Be sure to prewash both the towels and trim before beginning the project. (Fig. 8-10)

Fig. 8-10 Turn plain towels into lacy sensations by adding a special touch.

Materials Needed

♦ Purchased towels

♦ Wide lace with one decorative edge, the width of the towel plus 1"

♦ 1/2"- to 5/8"-wide satin ribbon the same length as the lace

♦ Matching machine-embroidery thread

How-Tos

For each towel:

1. Make a 1/4" double hem on both short ends of the lace.

2. Center the lace at the bottom edge of the towel with the decorative edge extending just below the towel edge.

3. Top-stitch the sides and straight edge of the lace to the towel. (Fig. 8-11)

Fig. 8-11 Finish the lace ends before top-stitching it to the towel and decoratively top-stitching ribbon over the upper edge.

4. Center and top-stitch both edges of the ribbon over the straight edge of the lace, sewing the same direction and tucking under both ends 1/2". Use a decorative machine stitch and machine-embroidery thread for more distinctive top-stitching.

Decorative Options

♦ Top-stitch a satin or grosgrain ribbon over the towel's woven band, tucking the ends under 1/2". Center a machine-embroidery motif over the ribbon. (Fig. 8-12)

♦ Pipe the long edges of a printed fabric band and top-stitch it over the towel's woven band, tucking the ends under 1/2".

♦ Bind the ends of the towel and add a matching appliqué on one end, centered over the border.

Fig. 8-12 Use your ingenuity to create a sensational gift.

SCENTED SOAP IN A SACK

This sweet-smelling gift hangs in a closet to freshen the clothes or gets tucked into a lingerie drawer. The soap inside can be used and replaced with another bar or with potpourri. (Fig. 8-13)

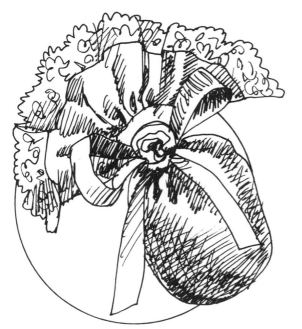

Fig. 8-13 Here's a double-duty gift—scented soap and a pretty sachet.

Materials Needed

♦ 1/6 yard of moiré taffeta or heavy rayon faille

♦ 1/2 yard of 1/2"-wide ruffled lace

♦ 2/3 yard of 3/8"-wide satin ribbon

♦ One ribbon rosette

♦ One bar of scented soap

Cutting Directions

♦ Cut two 4" by 6" fabric rectangles for the sack.

♦ Cut one 4" by 18" fabric rectangle for the ruffle.

How-Tos

Sew or serge all seams using 1/4" allowances.

1. Round both corners on one short end of the smaller rectangles. Fold the ribbon in half crosswise and place the fold on the right side of one rectangle 1" from the uncurved end. (Fig. 8-14)

2. Place the two smaller rectangles right sides together with the cut edges matching. Sew around the sides and rounded edges to form the bag, being careful not to catch the ribbon's loose ends in the stitching.

3. To form the fabric ruffle, sew the remaining rectangle into a circle with right sides together. Fold the circle in half lengthwise, wrong sides together, and press.

4. Fold one lace end under 1/2". Lap the fabric ruffle's pressed edge over the lace edge, matching the lace fold to the ruffle seamline. Top-stitch the ruffle to the lace, lapping the lace end 1/2" under the folded end.

5. Gather the fabric ruffle's lower edges to fit the upper bag edge. With right sides together, sew the ruffle to the bag.

6. Insert the soap and tie the ribbon around the bag, tying it with a bow. Hand-sew the rosette over the center of the bow.

Decorative Options

♦ Before constructing the sack, cover the fabric with decorative machine stitching for a sumptuous look.

♦ Make a set of three soap sacks in different colors for a more elaborate gift.

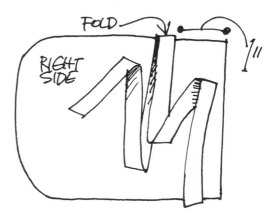

Fig. 8-14 Position the ribbon tie on one bag section before seaming the sides and lower edge.

CURL-SAVING PILLOWCASE

Both luxurious and practical, this satin pillowcase lets hair slide freely to protect curls and keep the styling in place. A safe, concealed zipper holds the case firmly on the pillow. (Fig. 8-15)

Fig. 8-15 Give someone carefree dreams with this hairdo-protecting pillowcase.

Materials Needed

♦ For a standard pillowcase: 5/8 yard of 60"-wide washable satin (or 1-2/3 yards of 45"-wide for two)

♦ For one or two queen-size pillowcases: 1-7/8 yards of 45"-wide or wider washable satin

♦ For one or two king-size pillowcases: 2-1/4 yards of 45"-wide or wider washable satin

♦ One 20" zipper with a polyester coil for each case

Cutting Directions

♦ For a standard pillowcase, cut one 21" by 60" rectangle.

♦ For a queen-size pillowcase, cut one 21" by 68" rectangle.

♦ For a king-size pillowcase, cut one 21" by 80" rectangle.

How-Tos

Sew or serge all seams using 1/4" allowances.

1. On one short end of the rectangle, press 1-1/2" to the wrong side. On the other short end, press 1/2" to the wrong side.

2. On the 1-1/2" allowance, center the zipper face down with the edge of the zipper tape matching the cut edge of the allowance, creating the zipper overlap. Using a zipper foot, top-stitch next to the zipper teeth on the right-hand side of the tape. (Fig. 8-16)

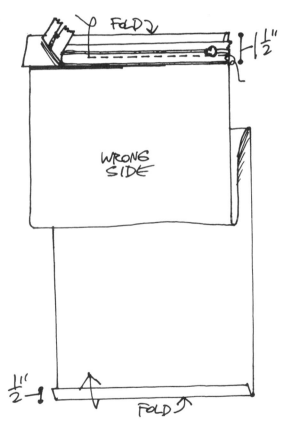

Fig. 8-16 Top-stitch the zipper to the wider fabric fold to create an overlap.

3. Fold the other pressed edge over the other side of the zipper tape, about 1/8" from the zipper teeth with both right side up. Top-stitch the folded edge to the tape.

4. Turn the pillowcase wrong side out. Fold the case so the folded edge of the zipper overlap is 3" away from one end. Open the zipper partially for later turning. Sew both long edges of the case, then turn it right side out and press. (Fig. 8-17)

Decorative Options

♦ Lap and top-stitch soft scalloped-edge lace to the edge of the pillowcase, turning under the top end of the lace before applying it.

♦ Machine-embroider or monogram the pillowcase to personalize it.

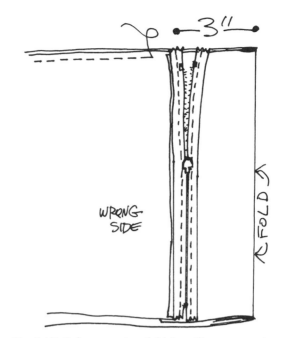

Fig. 8-17 Before seaming, fold the pillowcase so the edge of the overlap is 3" from one end.

SACHET DRAWER LINERS AND HANG-UPS

Although a favorite friend can use these scented wardrobe accessories at home, she will love them when she's on the go, too. They'll keep her clothes fresh smelling in suitcases, hotel-room drawers, and musty closets. (Fig. 8-18)

Fig. 8-18 What gift could be sweeter? Make these simple fragrant treasures.

Materials Needed

♦ 1/3 yard of 45"-wide fabric, such as satin or taffeta

♦ 1/3 yard of 45"-wide lace fabric

♦ One 12" by 18" piece of tulle for the drawer liner

♦ Two yards 1"-wide ruffled lace for the drawer liner

♦ 1-1/4 yards of 2"-wide flat lace with one scalloped edge for the hang-up

♦ 15" of 3/8"-wide ribbon for the drawer liner

♦ 22" of 1/4"-wide ribbon for the hang-up

♦ One ribbon rosette

♦ One bag of potpourri

Cutting Directions

For the drawer liner:

♦ Cut one 12" by 18" fabric rectangle for the bottom.

♦ Cut one 12" by 18" lace-fabric rectangle for the top.

For the heart-shaped hang-up:

♦ Cut two fabric hearts following the pattern grid.

♦ Cut one lace-fabric heart. (Fig. 8-19)

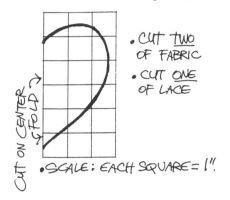

Fig. 8-19 The heart pattern includes 1/4" seam allowances.

How-Tos

Serge or sew all seams using 1/4" allowances.

For the drawer liner:

1. Seam the 1"-wide ruffled lace right sides together to the fabric rectangle, matching the cut edges and rounding the corners slightly as you sew. Finish by turning one end of the lace 1/2" to the wrong side and lapping 1/2" over the beginning fold.

2. Layer the lace-fabric rectangle right sides together over the fabric and place the tulle rectangle on top. Sew around all four edges, leaving an opening for turning and filling. (Fig. 8-20)

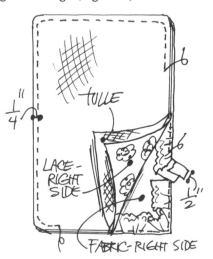

Fig. 8-20 Sew the outer edges of the liner, leaving an opening for turning.

3. Turn the liner right side out and fill it with potpourri between the fabric and the tulle. Hand-sew the opening closed.

> **Serger tip:** To eliminate turning, serge-seam the liner pieces wrong sides together, leaving an opening for filling. After adding the potpourri and serging the opening closed, topstitch the lace over the serged seam allowance.

4. Tie the 3/8"-wide ribbon into a bow and hand-sew it to one corner.

For the heart-shaped hang-up:

1. With both right side up, place the lace heart over one fabric heart. Pin the other fabric heart, right sides together, to the lace and fabric hearts. Sew around the outer edges, leaving an opening on one side for turning and filling. (Fig. 8-21)

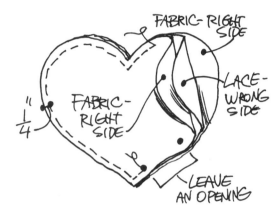

Fig. 8-21 Layer the lace and fabric before seaming and turning.

2. Turn the heart right side out with the lace on one side and fabric on the other. Press carefully. Insert the potpourri between the two fabric layers and hand-sew the opening closed.

> **Serger tip:** Serge-seam the hearts wrong sides together, beginning at the bottom point and pulling the edge straight at the upper center point as you serge over it. Leave an opening on the final long edge, put the potpourri between the two fabric layers, and serge-seam the opening closed.

3. Cut a 9" piece of the 1/4"-wide ribbon. Pin the cut edges together at the upper center point of the heart, lapping the ends 1/2" over the edge.

4. Machine-baste and gather the straight edge of the flat lace to fit the heart. Beginning at the lower point, top-stitch the lace around the edge of the heart over the gathering stitches. To finish, fold the end under 1/2" and lap it 1/2" over the beginning end.

5. Tie the remaining 1/4"-wide ribbon into a bow. Hand-sew it to the upper center point of the heart. Hand-sew the rosette over the center of the bow.

Decorative Options

♦ Substitute a less ornate fabric and trim. Consider chintz, calico, gingham, or a solid-color fabric in place of the satin, taffeta, and lace fabric. Trim with ruffled eyelet or a coordinating braid.

♦ If you're familiar with heirloom sewing, use those techniques to construct fabric for both projects.

LUXURIOUS PADDED HANGERS

Anyone can use more good hangers. These deluxe models protect clothes by preventing snags and shoulder stretching. Make them in a variety of colors or match someone's decor. (Fig. 8-22)

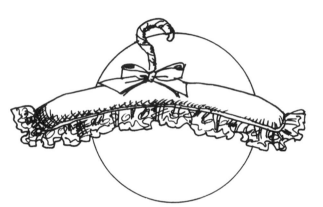

Fig. 8-22 Make a set of padded hangers that are both pretty and practical.

Materials Needed

For one hanger:
♦ 1/2 yard of fabric, such as satin, taffeta, or chintz (add an additional 3" for each additional hanger)

♦ One 8" by 20" rectangle of heavy batting

♦ One yard of 5/8"-wide ribbon

♦ 1-1/4 yards of 1"-wide ruffled lace with one straight edge

♦ One wooden hanger with a screw-in metal hook

♦ Glue gun and glue

Cutting Directions

Cut one 3" by 18" bias rectangle from the fabric.

How-Tos

1. Remove the hook from the hanger. Apply glue the length of the hook and wrap 20" of the ribbon around it, lapping the edges to cover the metal.

2. Fold the batting in half lengthwise. Fold the double-layer batting over the bottom edge of the wooden hanger and pin tightly. Using a zipper foot, sew closely around the sides and upper hanger edge. Trim the seam allowances close to the stitching. (Fig. 8-23)

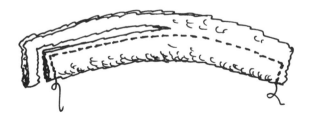

Fig. 8-23 Fold and sew the doubled batting over the hanger before trimming away the excess.

3. Fold the bias strip, right side out, over the top edge of the hanger and pin securely.

4. Using a zipper foot, seam the fabric close to the hanger, stretching both layers as you sew around the side and lower edges. Trim the seam allowances to 1/4". (Fig. 8-24)

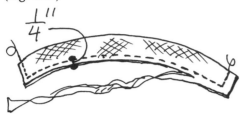

Fig. 8-24 Trim the seam allowance after sewing the bias fabric over the batting.

5. Starting at one end of the hanger, lap and hand-sew the lace straight edge over one side of the seam allowance then back around over the other side, enclosing the cut edges. Fold the finishing end 1/2" to the wrong side and lap it 1/2" over the beginning end.

6. Using the tip of your scissors, pierce a hole in the fabric over the hook placement. Screw the hook back into the hanger.

7. Tie the remaining ribbon into a bow around the base of the hook and hand-sew the knot to keep it from turning.

Decorative Options

♦ Hand-tack rosettes on the front of the hanger, 3" from each end, to hold straps securely on the hanger. (Fig. 8-25)

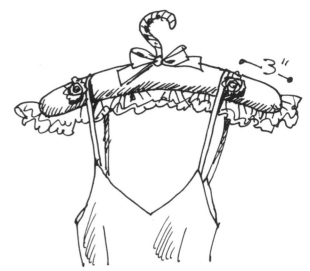

Fig. 8-25 Decorative rosettes keep straps on the hanger.

♦ Use *Ultrasuede* to cover the hanger. It has a nonslippery surface to keep clothes in place and, with a corded trim in place of the lace, makes a good man's gift as well.

PORTABLE DRESSER TRAY

Whether she's at home or away, this fold-up dresser tray will come in handy. She can pack or store it flat, then simply tie the ribbons at each corner to shape it for use. (Fig. 8-26)

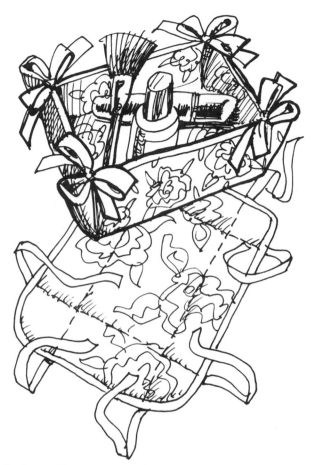

Fig. 8-26 Give a set of trays for a more elaborate gift—vary the dimensions as desired.

Materials Needed

♦ 1/4 yard of 45"-wide decorator fabric, such as a cotton/polyester print or tapestry

♦ One 9" by 10" rectangle of heavy fusible interfacing

♦ One 9" by 10" rectangle of fusible fleece

♦ 1-1/4 yards of 1/4"-wide cotton or polyester cording

♦ 1-1/4 yards of single-fold bias tape in a matching or coordinating color

♦ 2 yards of 3/8"-wide ribbon to match the bias tape

Cutting Directions

♦ Cut two 9" by 10" fabric rectangles.

♦ Cut the interfacing and fleece to the exact measurements given under Materials Needed.

How-Tos

1. Fuse the interfacing to the wrong side of one fabric rectangle for the outside of the box. Fuse the fleece to the wrong side of the other fabric rectangle for the inside of the box. Round the corners of both rectangles.

2. Make the piping by pressing the bias tape open and flat. Fold the tape snugly around the cording and, using a zipper foot, straight-stitch close to the cording edge.

3. Sew the piping to the right side of the rectangle that has the fleece on the underside. Begin in the center of one short end, matching the cut edges. Using a zipper foot, sew close to the piping, leaving a 1/4" seam allowance. Begin by tapering the piping onto the edge and finish by overlapping and tapering off. (Fig. 8-27)

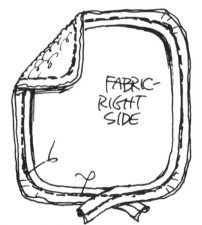

Fig. 8-27 Taper the piping on and off the edge, overlapping the ends.

4. Cut the ribbon into four equal pieces. On the right side of the interfaced rectangle, pin the ends of each piece 2" from each adjoining corner with the cut edges matching. (Fig. 8-28)

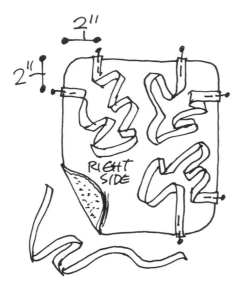

Fig. 8-28 Pin the ribbon ends to the box corners.

5. Place the two rectangles right sides together with the ribbon sandwiched between. Using a zipper foot, sew over the previous stitching from the piping application, leaving an opening for turning on one long side. Make certain not to catch the ribbon loops in the stitching.

6. Turn the tray right side out and press carefully. Hand- or machine-sew the opening closed. Cut each ribbon loop diagonally at the center point to form eight ties.

7. Mark and straight-stitch parallel lines across the tray in both directions, connecting the ribbon placements. (Fig. 8-29)

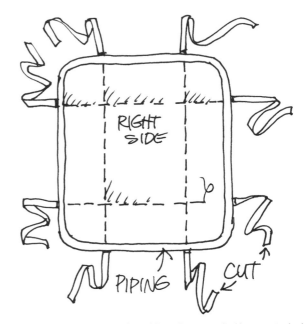

Fig. 8-29 After cutting the ribbon loops in half, top-stitch the lines for folding the box.

8. With the fleece side up, fold the tray on the stitching lines and press. Tie the ribbons into bows at each corner, pulling up the tray sides.

Decorative Options

♦ Instead of the piping, use ruffled lace or eyelet.

♦ Glue pearls or other beading around the tray edges after completing it without piping.

♦ Decoratively serge-finish the edges, wrong sides together, with the ribbon ties positioned right sides together over the interfacing side.

BULLETIN-BOARD ACCESSORY CENTER

Turn a purchased bulletin board into an efficient accessory display for a dressing room or bedroom wall. The elastic strips and pushpins exhibit bracelets, necklaces, pins, rings, and earrings. The lower pocket stores gloves, belts, and shoulder pads. (Fig. 8-30)

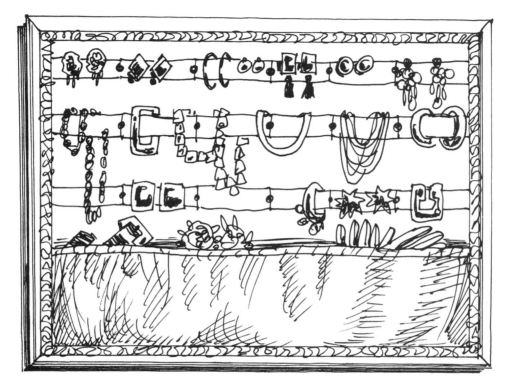

Fig. 8-30 No more hunting through drawers and jewelry boxes—this accessory organizer puts them all at her fingertips.

Materials Needed

♦ One 18" by 24" framed cork bulletin board

♦ 2/3 yard of 45"-wide or wider fabric for the background and pocket

♦ 2-1/2 yards of 3/4"-wide flexible decorative braid to cover the edges

♦ 3/4 yard of 3/8"-wide elastic for the pocket

♦ 2 yards of 1"-wide braided elastic for the cross straps

♦ Glue gun and glue

♦ Staple gun

♦ At least 15 pushpins

Cutting Directions

♦ Cut the fabric to the exact inside-frame measurements of the bulletin board.

♦ Cut one 12" by 30" fabric rectangle for the pocket.

♦ Cut the braided elastic into three 24" sections.

How-Tos

1. Position the elastic sections horizontally across the larger fabric rectangle without stretching them and with the top edges of the elastic 1", 4", and 8" from the top edge of the fabric. Top-stitch the elastic to the fabric on both ends and again every 4". (Fig. 8-31)

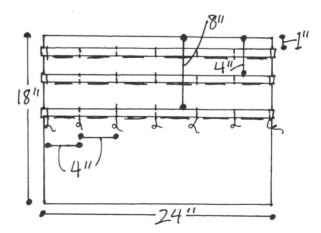

Fig. 8-31 Top-stitch the elastic straps to the fabric before stapling it to the board.

2. Put the fabric on the front of the bulletin board and staple it around all four outer edges, stretching firmly. Center a pushpin over each section of top-stitching on the elastic strips (they can be used to hold rings or chains). **Note:** Because cork boards vary, test the straps by slipping a bracelet underneath. If the pushpins come out, staple vertically under the pushpins or put two pushpins at every top-stitching location.

3. Fold the pocket in half lengthwise with the wrong sides together. Top-stitch a casing 1/2" from the folded edge.

4. Thread the 3/8" elastic into the casing, top-stitching across one end when it is even with the edge and pulling the opposite end until the pocket top is taut when held in position on the board. Top-stitch along the second edge to secure and trim the excess elastic close to the stitching. (Fig. 8-32)

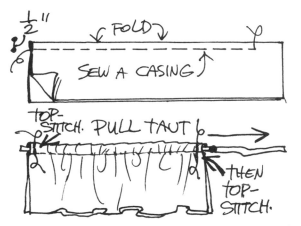

Fig. 8-32 Trim the excess elastic after gathering the pocket top.

5. Machine-baste and evenly gather the opposite long edge of the pocket. Staple the pocket securely along the side and bottom edges of the bulletin board, stretching the elastic to fit.

6. Glue the braid just inside the frame, covering the staples and raw edges. For the neatest corners, use a separate braid section for each side, turning under each end at least 1/4".

Decorative Options

♦ Gather both long edges of a matching or coordinating fabric strip to cover the bulletin board frame. Glue a same-size piece of batting over the frame. Then turn under and glue the gathered seam allowances to the frame edges, working the fabric around the corners and turning under the finishing end.

♦ Use a rigid lingerie lace instead of the braided elastic and top-stitch a matching row along the upper edge of the pocket.

CHAPTER NINE
Gifts for People on the Go

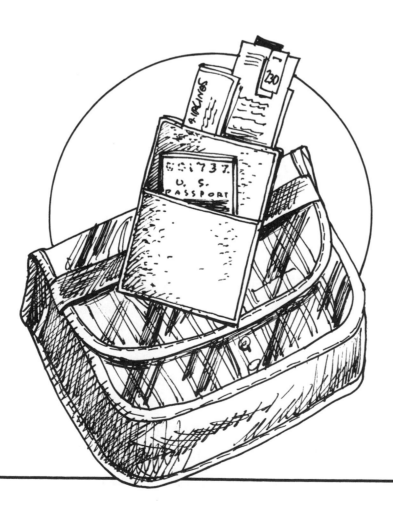

TRAVEL DOCUMENT CARRIER

Any frequent flyer will love this slim-design organizer for essential travel documents. A passport fits in the front pocket while tickets and itinerary information slip into the larger pocket. (Fig. 9-1)

Fig. 9-1 Lined *Ultrasuede* gives the case an elegant appearance.

Materials Needed

♦ 5" length of *Ultrasuede*

♦ 1/6 yard of 45"-wide taffeta for the lining

♦ 5" of heavy fusible interfacing

Cutting Directions

Cut one 13" by 5" rectangle and one 8" by 5" rectangle of the *Ultrasuede,* taffeta, and interfacing.

How-Tos

1. Fuse the interfacing to the wrong side of the *Ultrasuede.* To avoid flattening the *Ultrasuede* nap, place it right side down on a heavy terry towel while fusing.

2. Place the two large rectangles of *Ultrasuede* and taffeta right sides together and sew around them, using a 1/4" seam allowance and leaving an opening on one long edge for turning. For the neatest finish, sew from the interfacing side, allowing the taffeta edges to extend slightly beyond the *Ultrasuede.* Trim the corners and cut the seam allowances down to 1/8". Turn and press carefully, rolling the seam slightly toward the taffeta side.

3. Repeat step 2 for the other *Ultrasuede* and taffeta rectangles, but leave one short end open. After trimming and turning wrong sides together, edge-stitch the opening closed.

4. Edge-stitch across the opposite end of the smaller rectangle, turning at the corners and extending down the long edges for 3/4". Edge-stitch one end of the larger rectangle to match, then edge-stitch straight across the opposite end. (Fig. 9-2)

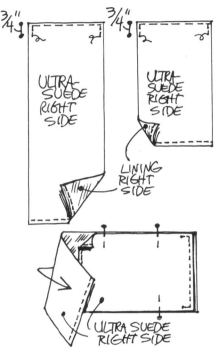

Fig. 9-2 Edge-stitch the two rectangles before assembling the carrier.

5. Align and pin the two rectangles wrong sides together with the matching edge-stitched ends and corners at the top edge of the carrier. At the lower edge of the shorter rectangle, fold up the remainder of the larger rectangle to form the pocket.

6. Edge-stitch across the lower edge of the carrier, catching the raw edges of the smaller pocket in the stitching. Edge-stitch up both sides through all layers, ending and back-stitching at the previous stitching so slits are created at the top edge.

Decorative Options

♦ Sew a monogram on one end of the longer rectangle before beginning step 1.

♦ Select a heavy woven fabric such as tapestry and decoratively serge-seam the lining and fabric wrong sides together instead of trimming and turning.

ROLL-UP IRONING BOARD

Pressing tricky sleeves and garment shoulders can be difficult on a flat surface in a hotel or dorm room. This nifty travel accessory includes a fold-out extension that functions as a sleeve board for top-notch results. (Fig. 9-3)

Fig. 9-3 Matching or coordinating binding holds the ironing board layers together.

Materials Needed

♦ 2/3 yard of 45"-wide decorative cotton/polyester fabric (or 1/2 yard of 60"-wide)

♦ 2/3 yard of 39"-wide cotton unbleached muslin

♦ 2/3 yard of 45"-wide *Teflon*-coated fabric (or 1/2 yard of 60"-wide)

♦ 2/3 yard of 60"-wide fusible fleece

♦ 4-1/4 yards of extrawide double-fold bias tape

♦ 1-1/2 yards of 5/8"-wide grosgrain ribbon to match the bias tape

Cutting Directions

♦ Cut one 18" by 30" and one 20" by 6" rectangle of the decorative fabric.

♦ Cut one 18" by 30" and one 20" by 6" rectangle of the muslin.

♦ Cut two 18" by 30" and two 20" by 6" rectangles of the fusible fleece.

♦ Cut one 18" by 30" and one 20" by 6" rectangle of the *Teflon*-coated fabric.

How-Tos

1. Fuse same-size fleece rectangles to the wrong sides of all the muslin and decorative fabric rectangles.

2. Layer the larger rectangles fleece sides together with the *Teflon*-coated rectangle sandwiched between, silver side toward the muslin. Repeat for the smaller rectangles.

3. Round all four corners of the larger rectangles and only the corners on one short end of the smaller rectangles.

4. Cut the ribbon into two 27" strips. Place the midpoint of each strip over the decorative fabric at one short end of the larger rectangles about 4" in from each side. Zigzag-baste all of the edges together on both rectangles, catching the ribbon folds in the stitching on the larger one. (Fig. 9-4)

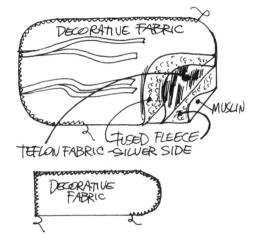

Fig. 9-4 The zigzagging compresses the layers for easier binding.

5. Using the bias trim, bind the smaller rectangle up one long edge, around the rounded end, and back down the opposite long edge to form the sleeve board.

6. Center the sleeve board, muslin side up on both rectangles, on the short end of the larger ironing-board rectangle opposite the end with the ribbons.

7. Beginning on one long edge, apply two-step binding to all edges of the ironing board, enclosing the sleeve board cut edges and the folded ends of the ribbon on the underside. Begin by folding under 1/2" and lap the end 1/2" over the beginning fold. (Fig. 9-5)

> **Serger tip:** In place of binding, decoratively serge-finish all edges using a wide, short, balanced 3-thread stitch and decorative thread, such as pearl cotton or crochet thread, in both loopers.

8. Roll up the ironing board and tie it with the ribbons.

Decorative Options

♦ Whip up other travel accessories, such as simple shoe bags, in a matching print.

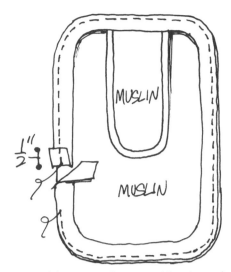

Fig. 9-5 Bind the outer edges, attaching the end of the sleeve board with the binding.

♦ Make an ironing board using school colors as a gift for someone on the way to college.

SEE-THROUGH TRAVEL ENVELOPES

You'll help anyone pack more efficiently with these moisture-resistant bags. Sweaters fit easily into the larger size and the smaller one is perfect for shirts. (Fig. 9-6)

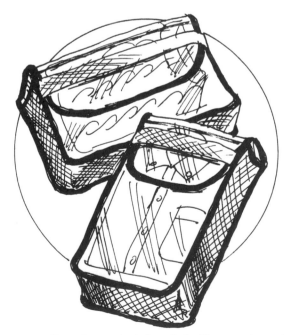

Fig. 9-6 The nylon pack cloth and vinyl bags are bound with grosgrain ribbon.

Materials Needed

♦ 2/3 yard of 60"-wide nylon pack cloth (add 5/8 yard for each additional sweater envelope and 1/2 yard for each extra shirt envelope)

♦ 3/8 yard of clear mediumweight vinyl (add 3/8 yard for each additional sweater envelope and 1/3 yard for each extra shirt envelope)

♦ 7-3/4 yards of 5/8"-wide grosgrain ribbon (add 4 yards for each additional sweater envelope and 3-3/4 yards for each extra shirt envelope)

Cutting Directions

For the sweater envelope:
♦ Cut one envelope back from the fabric following the pattern grid. (Fig. 9-7)

♦ Cut one 13" by 16" rectangle from the vinyl.

♦ Cut one 3" by 42" fabric strip for the envelope gusset.

♦ Cut one 3" by 16" fabric strip for band.

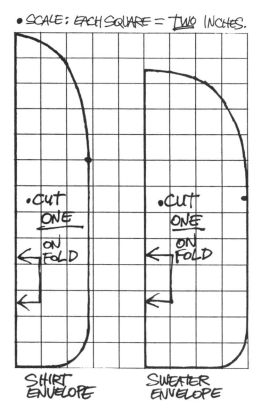

• SCALE: EACH SQUARE = TWO INCHES.

• CUT ONE ON FOLD

• CUT ONE ON FOLD

SHIRT ENVELOPE   SWEATER ENVELOPE

Fig. 9-7 Cut one of pack cloth for each bag.

For the shirt envelope:

♦ Cut one envelope back from the fabric following the pattern grid. (See Fig. 9-7)

♦ Cut one 11-1/2" by 16" rectangle from the vinyl.

♦ Cut one 3" by 42" fabric strip for the gusset.

♦ Cut one 3" by 11-1/2" fabric strip for the band.

How-Tos

The instructions are generally the same for both sizes of envelope.

1. Fold the band strip in half lengthwise with right sides together. Seam the long cut edges using a 1/4" allowance. Turn the band right side out and press lightly. For the sweater envelope, fold and press the seam to the center of the underside and place the band on the vinyl rectangle 3" from one long edge. (The shirt envelope opens from the end, so position its band 3" from one short end.) Machine-baste the band ends in position using a medium-length and medium-width zigzag stitch. (Fig. 9-8)

2. With the wrong side of the vinyl on the wrong side of the gusset fabric, machine-baste the gusset to the vinyl sides and lower edge using a long, medium-width zigzag stitch. Begin at the upper right corner above the band end. Ease the gusset to the vinyl, rounding the corners and catching the band ends in

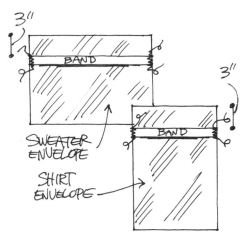

Fig. 9-8 Position the bands on the vinyl fronts.

the stitching. Continue to the opposite upper corner of the vinyl and trim any extra gusset fabric when you reach the vinyl upper edge.

3. Press the ribbon exactly in half lengthwise for the binding. Fold the pressed ribbon over the zigzagged edges and top-stitch along the ribbon edge, being sure to catch the other ribbon edge on the underside.

4. Following the instructions in step 3, bind the remaining vinyl edge and the gusset ends, folding the previous binding toward the vinyl. (Fig. 9-9)

5. Position the envelope back and gusset wrong sides together, matching the gusset end to the pattern markings. Zigzag-baste the back and gusset together, using the techniques in step 2.

6. Beginning at the center bottom of the envelope, bind continuously around the outer edges. End by folding the ribbon 1/2" to the wrong side and lapping it over the beginning end for 1/2".

7. Fold down the flap and tuck it under the band.

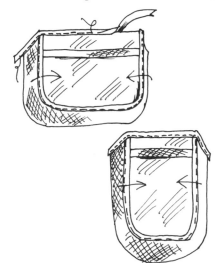

Fig. 9-9 Fold the first binding toward the bag center before binding the upper edge.

AUDIOCASSETTE CASE

Although cassette tapes are not the latest musical invention, many people on your gift list still play them in their car. This nifty case keeps the tapes organized and easy to select. (Fig. 9-10)

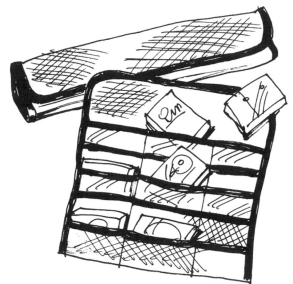

Fig. 9-10 Nine cassettes fit inside this fold-up organizer.

Materials Needed

♦ 1/2 yard of nylon pack cloth

♦ 3" of medium- to heavyweight clear vinyl

♦ 3-3/4 yards of 5/8"-wide grosgrain ribbon

♦ 2" of 3/4"-wide *Velcro*

Cutting Directions

♦ Cut two 16" by 19-1/2" rectangles from the pack cloth.

♦ Cut two 3" by 16" pockets from the vinyl.

How-Tos

1. Place the pack-cloth rectangles wrong sides together. Round the corners on one short end for the case flap.

2. Cut the *Velcro* into two equal lengths. Top-stitch the hooked *Velcro* sections near the curved end of one rectangle, 1/2" from the top edge and 4" in from each side.

3. On the other rectangle, place a marking 10-1/2" down from the curved edge and 4" in from each side. Sew a looped *Velcro* section at each marking. (Fig. 9-11)

4. Press the grosgrain ribbon exactly in half lengthwise. Fold the ribbon over both long edges of

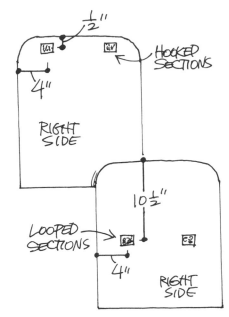

Fig. 9-11 Top-stitch the *Velcro* to the pack cloth before applying the pockets and binding.

the two vinyl pockets and top-stitch to bind them, being sure both edges are caught in the stitching.

5. Place the two pack-cloth rectangles wrong sides together and bind the straight short end using the technique in step 4.

6. Place one vinyl pocket 6" from the bound straight edge. (Pin in the seam allowance only to prevent making holes in the vinyl.) Top-stitch over the binding across the lower edge of the pocket.

7. Place the other vinyl pocket 2" above the upper edge of the other vinyl pocket. Top-stitch along the lower edge. (Fig. 9-12)

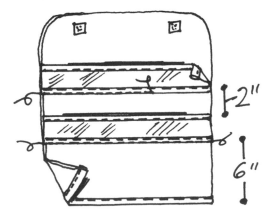

Fig. 9-12 Position the vinyl pockets and top-stitch the lower edges to the case.

8. Bind the sides and upper curved edge of the case, beginning and ending at the lower corners. Fold 1/2" of the ribbon to the wrong side on each end before stitching over it.

9. Fold up the lower edge 2-1/2" to form another row of pockets. Top-stitch through the binding on each side to hold the pockets in position.

10. Mark three parallel vertical stitching lines approximately 5-1/4" apart. Top-stitch on the lines, beginning at the lower edge and sewing to the top of the upper pocket. Back-stitch at both ends to secure. (For ease in top-stitching over the vinyl, use a plastic or roller foot. Or place a layer of tissue paper over the case, mark and sew the lines on the paper, and tear away the paper afterward.)

> **Serger tip:** Instead of binding, serge-finish the lower and outer edges using decorative thread, such as crochet thread or pearl cotton, in the loopers. Use a wide, satin-length, balanced 3-thread stitch.

11. Put a special new cassette in one of the pockets as an extra gift. Roll up the case and close it with the *Velcro* tabs.

Decorative Options

♦ Machine-embroider a name or initials on the outside of the flap.

♦ For elegance, fuse heavy interfacing to the back of a piece of *Ultrasuede* and use it instead of the pack cloth.

PORTABLE CLOTHING VALET

This hang-up travel helper organizes underwear, socks, and other accessories in addition to pajamas and folded clothing. It hangs in a garment bag or folds up in a suitcase. (Fig. 9-13)

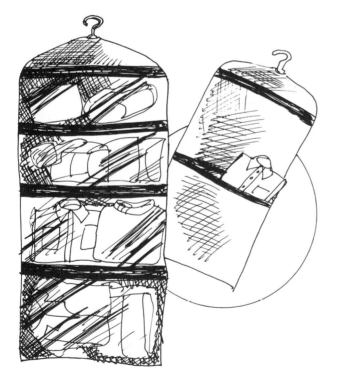

Fig. 9-13 They'll never have to dig through a suitcase when everything they need is hanging in clear view.

Materials Needed

♦ 1-1/8 yards of 60"-wide nylon pack cloth

♦ 1/2 yard of mediumweight clear vinyl

♦ Six 18" zippers

♦ 6-1/2 yards of 7/8"-wide grosgrain ribbon

♦ One hanger

Cutting Directions

♦ Cut two 19" by 40" rectangles for the valet and two 19" by 16" rectangles for pockets from the pack cloth.

♦ Cut two 19" by 6" rectangles and two 19" by 10-1/2" pockets from the vinyl.

How-Tos

Serge or sew all seams using 3/8" allowances.

1. Place the two large pack-cloth rectangles wrong sides together and trace around the top edge of a hanger at one short end, adding a 3/8" seam allowance. Cut on the marked line. (When using fabric other than pack cloth, zigzag-finish the hanger opening on both pieces.)

2. Press the ribbon exactly in half lengthwise. Bind one long edge of a fabric pocket. With right sides up, place the pocket on the lower edge of one valet rectangle, matching the cut edges. Machine-baste the lower edges together.

3. Lap and top-stitch the upper pocket edge over the right side of one zipper, approximately 1/8" from the zipper teeth. Machine-baste the side and lower edges.

4. Bind both long edges of the other fabric pocket. Lap one edge over the other side of the zipper. Top-stitch approximately 1/8" from the zipper teeth, stitching through all layers. (Fig. 9-14)

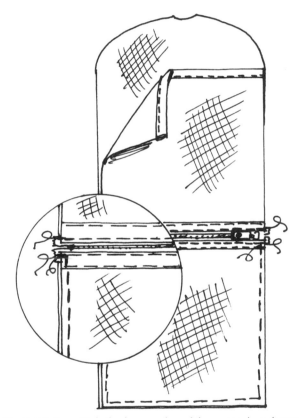

Fig. 9-14 Top-stitch the lower edge of the second pocket to the zipper tape and the pack-cloth rectangle.

5. Lap the other edge of the pocket over another zipper and top-stitch. (Do not stitch it to the valet rectangle.)

6. Bind the other edge of the zipper tape.

7. Top-stitch the bound zipper tape to the valet rectangle, close to the folded edge. (Fig. 9-15)

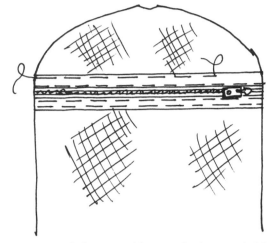

Fig. 9-15 Finish the upper fabric pocket by top-stitching the bound zipper tape to the backing.

8. Repeat steps 2 through 5 twice on the right side of the other valet rectangle for the four vinyl pockets, beginning with the two larger pockets on the lower part of the valet and positioning the two smaller pockets above. Then repeat steps 6 and 7.

9. Place the right sides of the two valet rectangles together and seam around the edges, leaving an opening at the top for the hanger hook and a larger opening on one long side edge for turning and inserting the hanger.

10. Trim the corners and turn the valet right side out. Insert the hanger and hand-stitch the side opening closed.

GLOVE-COMPARTMENT ORGANIZER

Help someone end glove-compartment clutter with this roomy fold-up case. It holds pens, tools, maps, and insurance information. (Fig. 9-16)

Fig. 9-16 This sturdy case keeps small auto accessories neatly organized.

Materials Needed

1/3 yard of 60"-wide nylon pack cloth

One 4-1/2" by 3-1/2" rectangle of clear lightweight vinyl

1-2/3 yards of 5/8"-wide grosgrain ribbon

2" of 3/4"-wide *Velcro*

Cutting Directions

From the pack cloth:

♦ Cut two 14" by 10" rectangles for the organizer base.

Cut one 14" by 12" rectangle for the larger pocket.

Cut one 3" by 10" rectangle for the pencil pocket.

Cut one 4-1/2" by 10" rectangle for the middle pocket.

How-Tos

Serge or sew all seams using 1/4" allowances.

1. Press the larger pocket in half lengthwise, wrong sides together.

2. Press the ribbon exactly in half lengthwise. Use it to bind one long edge of the vinyl, top-stitching along the ribbon edge and catching the underlayer in the stitching. Then turn under 1/2" on one end of the remaining ribbon and bind the left-hand short end of the vinyl, covering the raw edge of the first binding. (The other two sides will be covered by the outer binding of the organizer.)

3. Place the bound vinyl on the lower right corner of the larger pocket, matching the raw edges. Top-stitch the vinyl to the pocket by sewing over the previous stitching on the bound short end. (Fig. 9-17)

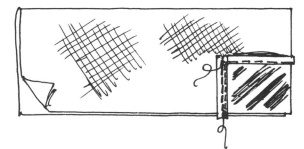

Fig. 9-17 Back-stitch at both ends when top-stitching the side of the vinyl pocket.

4. Fold the middle pocket in half crosswise with right sides together. Seam both long edges. Trim the corners, turn the pocket to the right side, and press carefully. Repeat for the pencil pocket.

5. Center the middle pocket over the larger pocket, matching the bottom edges. Top-stitch the two side edges, back-stitching at the ends.

6. Place the pencil pocket 1-3/4" from the left side of the larger pocket, aligning the lower edges. Top-stitch both long edges, back-stitching at the ends. Also top-stitch down the center of the pocket. (Fig. 9-18)

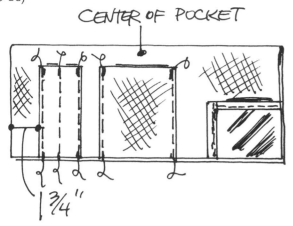

Fig. 9-18 Position and top-stitch the middle and pencil pockets on top of the larger pocket.

7. Cut the *Velcro* into two 1" lengths. Top-stitch one hooked section 1/2" from either side at the lower left corner of the larger pocket.

8. Place the pocket on the right side of one of the larger organizer-base rectangles, matching the lower edges. Machine-baste the cut edges to the base. Top-stitch the other hooked *Velcro* section in the upper left corner of the base, 1/2" from either edge.

9. On the right side of the remaining base rectangle, top-stitch the looped *Velcro* sections 3" from the left side and 1/2" from the upper and lower edges.

10. Place the two base rectangles wrong sides together. To divide the larger pocket, top-stitch parallel lines 4-3/4" from either end through all layers. (Fig. 9-19)

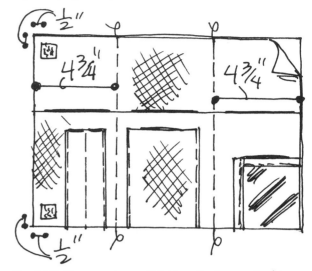

Fig. 9-19 The organizer will fold on the two vertical top-stitching lines.

11. Bind the outside edges with the remaining ribbon, following the instructions in step 2, turning under 1/2" and lapping each corner.

12. Fold the organizer on the two vertical stitching lines and close it with the *Velcro*.

Decorative Options

♦ Monogram the front flap of the organizer before applying the pockets.

♦ Make a matching Audiocassette Case, featured previously.

BEACH-CHAIR CADDY

Give a beach lover this handy carrier to hold all the essentials—even a folding chair. Two vinyl pockets make small items easy to find, but there's also a self-fabric pocket for privacy. (Fig. 9-20)

Fig. 9-20 They can carry a beach chair, towel, and three pockets full of fun-in-the-sun gear.

Materials Needed

♦ 1-7/8 yards of 60"-wide nylon pack cloth

♦ 2/3 yard clear mediumweight vinyl

♦ 2-1/4 yards of 1"-wide cotton or nylon webbing

♦ 5-3/4 yards of 5/8"-wide grosgrain ribbon

♦ 2-1/4 yards of 7/8"-wide grosgrain ribbon

♦ One 20" zipper

♦ Six gripper snaps

♦ 3" of 1-1/2"-wide *Velcro*

Cutting Directions

From the pack cloth:

♦ Cut two 48" by 24" rectangles for the caddy base.

♦ Cut one 20-1/2" by 18" rectangle for the pocket.

From the vinyl:

♦ Cut one 22" by 20" rectangle for the larger pocket.

♦ Cut one 8" by 18" rectangle for the smaller pocket.

How-Tos

Sew or serge all seams using 1/4" allowances.

1. On the pack-cloth pocket piece, press 1/2" to the wrong side on both short ends. Lap the folded edges over the opposite right sides of the zipper tape, approximately 1/8" from the teeth, and top-stitch without catching the pocket fabric underneath the zipper.

2. Open the zipper halfway. Fold the pocket, right sides together, with the zipper 1-1/2" from the top fold. Seam both sides. (Fig. 9-21)

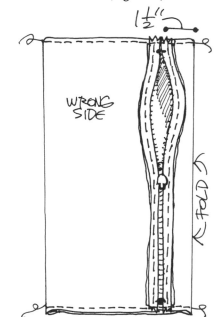

Fig. 9-21 Turn the pocket right side out through the partially opened zipper after seaming the sides.

3. Turn the pocket right side out through the zipper and press carefully with a warm iron. Center the pocket on the right side of one large rectangle with the upper pocket edge 10" from one short end. Top-stitch around all sides of the pocket.

4. Round the corners on one short end of both vinyl pocket rectangles. Press the narrower grosgrain ribbon exactly in half lengthwise. Fold the ribbon over the opposite unrounded short end of the larger vinyl rectangle and top-stitch to bind the edge, catching both layers of ribbon in the stitching.

5. Fold up the bound edge on the vinyl rectangle 7" to form a pocket. Beginning at the lower pocket edge, bind up one side, around the curved top, and down the other edge, turning under 1/2" at both ends. (Fig. 9-22)

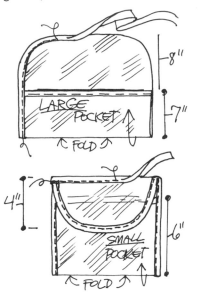

Fig. 9-22 Fold up 7" and bind the large pocket, then turn down a 6-1/2" flap. On the smaller pocket, turn up 6" at the bottom and fold down a 4" flap.

6. Fold the rounded end down 6-1/2" and bind the fold, following the procedure in step 5.

7. Top-stitch the sides and lower edge of the finished vinyl pocket to the rectangle, with the pocket top centered 9" down from the end opposite the zippered pocket. Then fold the pocket top down and top-stitch its upper bound edge to the rectangle.

8. Repeat steps 5 through 7 for the smaller pocket, folding up 6" for the pocket and down 4" for the top flap. Top-stitch the pocket 1/2" above the larger pocket, centering it between the side edges of the rectangle.

9. For a rolled-towel holder, cut the *Velcro* into three equal lengths. Cut three 10" lengths of the webbing. On each webbing strip, seam the wrong side of the hooked *Velcro* section to the right side of one end of the webbing. Fold the *Velcro* away from the webbing and the seam allowance toward it. Top-stitch through all layers, close to the webbing fold.

10. Fold and press-mark the pocketed rectangle in half crosswise, wrong sides together. Then fold it in half lengthwise and mark the center point and positions 3" from either side. Also mark points 2" above and below the center marks for the ends of the webbing straps. (Fig. 9-23)

11. Following the placement in Fig. 9-23, place the raw ends of the webbing straps on the three upper markings with the wrong sides up and extending toward the caddy's top edge. Top-stitch 1/4" from the webbing's cut edges.

12. Top-stitch the *Velcro* loop sections at the other markings.

13. Place the two caddy base rectangles wrong sides together and round the corners. With the cut edges matching, pin each end of the remaining webbing above the vinyl pockets, 2" from the side edges.

14. Press the wider ribbon exactly in half lengthwise. Starting at the center of one long side, bind the edges of the rectangle, being sure to catch both ribbon edges in the stitching. Finish by folding 1/2" to the wrong side and lapping it over the beginning end 1/2". Top-stitch over the webbing ends to reinforce the carrying strap.

15. Apply gripper snaps next to the binding at the corners. Center two more snaps between the corner ones at the upper edge. Also position one snap on each side of the caddy, 12" down from the upper edge (see Fig. 9-23).

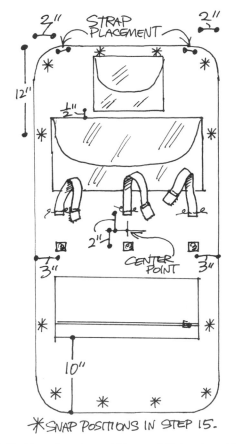

Fig. 9-23 Complete the webbing and *Velcro* towel holder before finishing the rest of the caddy.

TRAVEL TOILETRY TOTE

When traveling, anyone will love this tough, water-resistant bag to keep grooming supplies organized. With a zipper on three sides, the bag opens flat for easy accessibility while hanging from the bathroom door. (Fig. 9-24)

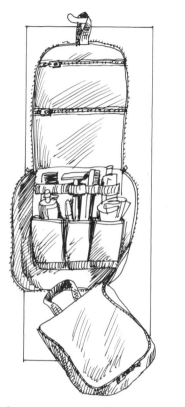

Fig. 9-24 All the conveniences of home are featured in this special travel tote.

Materials Needed

♦ 2/3 yard of 60"-wide pack cloth

♦ Two 18" zippers

♦ Two 9" zippers

♦ 1/3 yard of 5/8"-wide grosgrain ribbon

♦ 1/3 yard of 3/4"-wide elastic

♦ 20" of 1"-wide cotton or nylon webbing

Cutting Directions

♦ Cut one 20" by 10" pocket rectangle.

♦ Cut two base pieces. (Fig. 9-25)

♦ Cut two sides pieces.

♦ Cut three top pieces and trim 3/4" from the straight short ends of two of them.

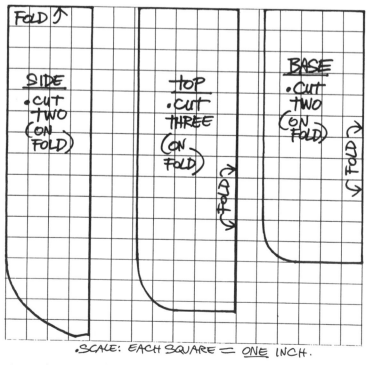

Fig. 9-25 Cut out these shaped pieces plus one 20" by 10" rectangle to make the travel tote.

How-Tos

1. Place the elastic on the right side of one base piece 2" from the straight short end. Trim the ends to fit and machine-baste the elastic 1/4" from the sides. Top-stitch vertically through the elastic, creating one 3" elastic section and several 1" and 1-1/2" sections.

2. Press the pocket rectangle in half lengthwise, wrong sides together, and edge-stitch 1/8" from the fold.

3. Place the pocket over the curved end of the base, both right side up. Match the cut edges on the sides but position the pocket 1" above the lower edge. Top-stitch the pocket to the base 1/2" from the side edges. Fold in and pin three sections across the pocket width. Straight-stitch between each pocket, being careful not to catch the pocket in the stitching. (Fig. 9-26)

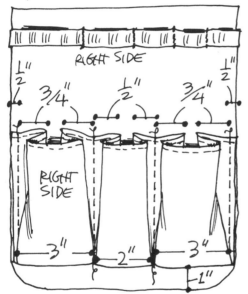

Fig. 9-26 Fold and stitch the pocket to the tote base.

4. Machine-baste the pocket to the base 1/4" from the lower pocket edge. Place the ribbon over the lower pocket edge, just lapping the machine-basting. Top-stitch it along both long edges.

5. On the longest top piece, cut horizontally on a line 2" below the curved short edge. Press 1/4" to the wrong side on both newly cut edges. Lap the folded edges over the right side of one 9" zipper, 1/8" from the zipper teeth, with the top of the zipper tape matching the left cut edge of the fabric. Top-stitch along the folds. (Use a zipper foot for all zipper applications in this project.)

6. Cut the piece again on a horizontal line 6" from the straight short end. Press 1/4" to the wrong side on both newly cut edges and insert the other 9" zipper as in step 5. Sew across the ends of the zippers 1/4" from the cut edges and trim them to match the cut edges. (Fig. 9-27)

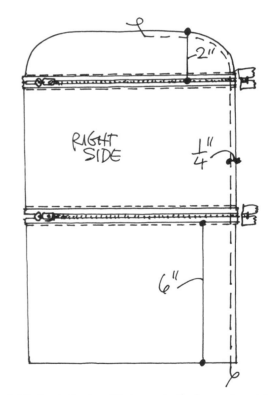

Fig. 9-27 Apply the two 9" zippers to the longer top section.

7. With the wrong side of the zippered top on the right side of one of the other top pieces, top-stitch 3/4" above the lower zipper. Machine-baste at 1/4" around all sides of the two pieces.

8. Fold one side section in half crosswise and mark the center of the long curved edge. Open one 18" zipper and place it right sides together against the side piece with the zipper top at the center marking and the edges matching. Sew the zipper to the side 1/8" away from the zipper teeth, beginning and ending 1/4" from each end. Repeat for the opposite side section half and the second zipper with the top edges meeting in the center. (Fig. 9-28)

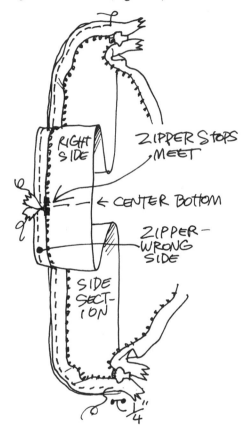

Fig. 9-28 Sew half of the two 18" zippers to the curved edge of the side section.

9. Place the two side pieces right sides together and stitch over the previous stitching.

10. Turn the side section right side out and press carefully. Place the wrong side of the zippered side section on the right side of the pocketed base piece, matching the cut edges on the sides and lower edges. Starting 1/4" from the top of the base, seam them together using a 1/4" allowance and easing the side section around the corners.

11. Place the two base pieces right sides together with the side section sandwiched between. Stitch over the previous stitching, beginning and ending 1/4" from the cut edges. (Fig. 9-29)

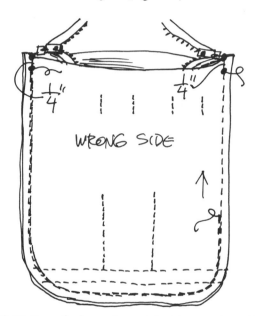

Fig. 9-29 Seam the base pieces right sides together with the side section in the middle.

12. Place the zippered top piece right sides together with the pocketed base, matching the straight short ends. Seam through the upper layer of the base and both layers of the top using a 1/4" allowance and being careful not to catch the bottom base piece in the stitching.

13. Mark the upper center of the remaining top piece. Place the unsewn zipper ends right sides together around the top, with the edges matching and the zipper ends meeting at the upper center of the top. Stitch 1/8" away from the zipper teeth. (Fig. 9-30)

14. Cut the webbing into two 10" pieces. Fold one piece in half for a hanging loop and pin it at the upper center over the zipper ends. With the tops right sides together, sew over the previous stitching, reinforcing the loop ends by stitching over them at least twice.

15. Position the remaining webbing for a carrying handle, matching the cut edges of the outside base and top with the webbing ends, 2" in from each side. Seam, leaving an opening between the webbing ends for turning.

16. Turn the tote right side out and press carefully, tucking the remaining cut edges to the inside. Top-stitch the opening closed.

17. Top-stitch around the entire tote 1/8" away from the zipper teeth.

Decorative Options

♦ Use a color-matched zipper and webbing to add a decorative accent to a contrasting fabric.

♦ Machine-monogram initials on the outer bag top piece before beginning step 13.

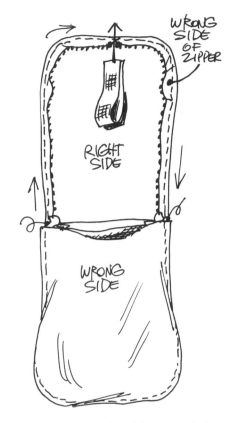

Fig. 9-30 Sew the other sides of the two 18" zippers to the remaining top piece before centering the webbing loop over the ends.

CHAPTER TEN
Wrapping It Up

Part of the fun of giving a special gift is presenting it with flair. And even the most charming wrappings don't need to be time-consuming or expensive. Your sewing skills and supplies can make the job a breeze.

Even at the last minute, you can substitute fabric for paper and ribbon. Bags and boxes can be made quickly. And as an added bonus–all of the wrapping materials can by recycled or put to other uses later. The ideas and directions presented in this chapter are only the beginning. Experiment, try unusual components and treatments, and show off your creativity.

Paper Substitutes

Fabric was used as gift wrap long before paper was widely available. Why not put your scraps, remnants, and expendable yardage to good use?

Simply cut the fabric to fit the size of the gift or gift box and finish the edges using pinking sheers, a double hem, or decorative serge-finishing.

Consider using squares of cotton or cotton/polyester that can double as napkins later–they can be any size, from a 12" to a 26" square. Or finish the edge of a rectangle or square of silk or silky fabric that can be reused as a scarf. The most common scarf sizes are 10" by 54" rectangles, 15" by 62" rectangles, or squares from 18" to 36".

You can tie a square or rectangle of fabric to cover a gift in several ways. Here are three of the easiest:

♦ **_Basic knotted wrap_**–Center the gift diagonally on the wrong side of the fabric. Fold two opposite corners over the center of the gift. Pull up and knot the two remaining corners on top. (Fig. 10-1)

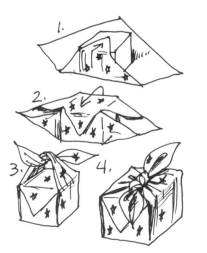

Fig. 10-1 For a basic knotted wrap, fold the first two corners and tie the remaining two.

♦ **_Double-knot wrap_**–Center the gift diagonally on the wrong side of the fabric. Pull up two opposite corners and knot them on top. Pull up the two remaining corners and knot them over the first knot. (Fig. 10-2)

Fig. 10-2 Tie both opposite corners to make a decorative double knot on top of the package.

♦ **_Popper wrap_**–Center the gift on the wrong side of the fabric, close to one edge. Fold that edge over the gift and roll to the opposite edge. Tie ribbon or cording bows to secure the remaining edges. (Fig. 10-3)

Fig. 10-3 Roll the fabric around a small gift and tie both ends like a popper.

Use a finished fabric circle as another gift-wrap option. Cut a single-layer circle with the diameter equal to the circumference of the gift plus at least 6". Serge-finish or pink the edges. Center the gift on the wrong side of the fabric, pull up the edges evenly, and tie cording or a ribbon around the fabric just above the gift. (Fig. 10-4)

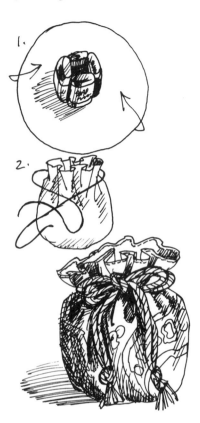

Fig. 10-4 Finish the edges of a fabric-circle wrap by pinking, serge-finishing, or sewing two layers together.

It is difficult to hem a round gift wrap on the sewing machine, but you can make a double-layer wrap with a neatly finished edge. Sew two equal-size circles right sides together, leaving an opening for turning. Trim the allowances, turn the fabric right side out, and press carefully, tucking the allowances on the opening to the inside. Edge-stitch around the circle.

Ribbon Substitutes

Cut strips of fabric to use as ribbon. Finish the edges, if desired, by pinking or serge-finishing. On lightweight fabrics, you may also choose to double hem the ribbon edges.

Serger tip: Ribbon edges serge-finished over fine wire can be formed into bows of almost any shape. Purchase lightweight beading wire, available in craft stores.

1. Adjust for a satin-length rolled-edge stitch or a satin-length, narrow- to medium-width, balanced 3-thread stitch with decorative thread in the upper looper of the rolled edge or in both loopers of the balanced stitch.

2. Place the wire under the back and over the front of a beading foot, rolled-edge foot, or standard presser foot. Serge SLOWLY over the wire for at least 1", guiding it carefully between the needle and the knives. Pull gently on the wire and thread behind the foot to guide it smoothly.

3. Raise the presser foot and position the end of one long fabric edge under the foot and wire. Serge slowly until some of the fabric clears the back of the presser foot. Then bend the wire end back over the fabric to anchor it. (Fig. 10-5)

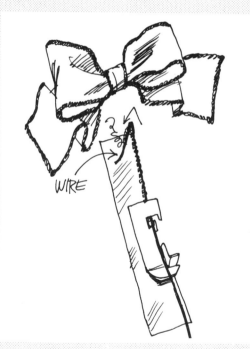

Fig. 10-5 Fold back the wire end to anchor it as you continue serging along the ribbon edge.

4. Serge off over the wire on the opposite end, cut a 1" tail, and bend it back.

5. Repeat steps 2 through 4 for the opposite long edge of the fabric strip. Serge-finish the ends to match, if desired, and tie the ribbon into a bow.

Quickly cut ribbon using a rotary cutter and mat. You have the option of cutting the ribbon strips crossgrain if the fabric width will be as wide as the length of ribbon you'll need. For strips longer than the fabric width, cut on the lengthwise grain using the amount of yardage desired.

Purchase a remnant with no visible right or wrong side or use fabric you have on hand. For convenience later, cut the entire piece into ribbon strips and wrap them around an empty spool.

1. Fold the fabric in half crosswise, lining up the selvages. Then fold crosswise again so you'll be cutting through four layers at a time. (Fig. 10-6)

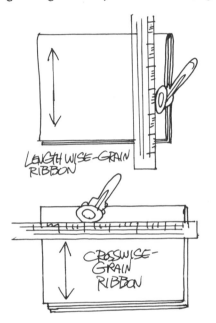

Fig. 10-6 Quickly cut ribbon four layers at a time.

2. Use a quilting ruler as a guide—a long 24" one works well. Position the ruler in the direction you will be cutting the strips. If the fabric isn't lined up evenly, cut off about 1/2" on the first edge to do so.

3. Aligning the cutting mat and the ruler, measure and cut strips the width you want the ribbon. If you are cutting the entire piece, you may choose to vary the ribbon widths for use on different packages. **Note:** Check each strip as you cut it. If it is not perfectly straight, the fabric has slipped and is not lined up. To correct this, cut another 1/2" from the edge before cutting the next ribbon strip.

If you will be pinking the ribbon edges, you won't need to use the rotary cutter first. Simply pink the first edge, then cut off long strips using the pinking shears. Choose gingham or another fabric with a definite stripe for the easiest pinked ribbon—you can follow the lines so marking isn't necessary.

Serger tip: Use your serger to cut and serge-finish one edge of the fabric strips simultaneously. Select a fabric with no visible right or wrong side or use two layers wrong sides together. Adjust for a rolled edge or narrow balanced stitch (decorative thread is optional). Serge on either the lengthwise or crosswise grain depending on the length of ribbon you want to make. Reverse the serging direction on the opposite long edge of each strip so the stitching will be uniform on both sides of the ribbon. (Fig. 10-7)

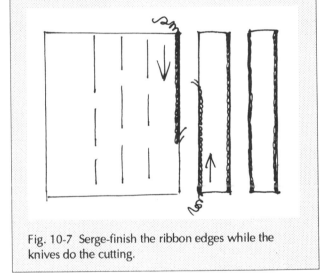

Fig. 10-7 Serge-finish the ribbon edges while the knives do the cutting.

If you prefer a stiffer ribbon, fuse two layers of fabric wrong sides together using fusible transfer web. Cut out the ribbon strips using any of the methods previously described. Two layers of contrasting fabric will give the ribbon an interesting two-sided effect.

For variety, try these additional sewing-related ribbon ideas:

♦ Instead of tying the ribbon, secure it on top of the package with a pull-through buckle or a scarf ring. As an additional gift, use a long rectangular scarf instead of the ribbon. (Fig. 10-8)

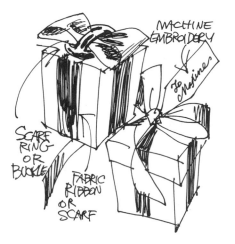

Fig. 10-8 Use your imagination to tie up packages with flair.

♦ Use your machine's programmed decorative stitches or letters to embroider the ribbon. Ribbon streamers with the recipient's name and a short message from you can function as a gift tag.

♦ Decorate the ribbon with fabric paint. Add rhinestones for a sparkling touch.

♦ To make curling ribbon, fuse gift wrapping paper to fabric. For best results, fuse the web to the fabric first, then use little or no steam while fusing the paper to the other side. Cut narrow ribbon strips and use scissors to curl them from the fabric side. (Fig. 10-9)

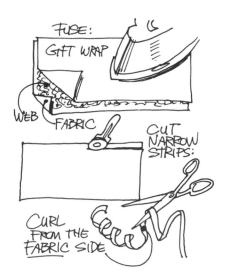

Fig. 10-9 Fuse fabric to gift wrap for narrow curling ribbon.

♦ Save leftover lengths of cording, satin and grosgrain ribbon, lace, braid, and other trim to wrap packages later.

♦ Tie a cloth tape measure around a small package.

Great Gift Bags

Make a fabric gift bag or box that can be used again and again. They are quick and easy, plus you'll use your fabric remnants constructively.

♦ Whip up speedy flat bags for bottles or any small gift.

1. Cut a fabric rectangle the bag height by twice the bag width. Add 1/2" in both directions for hemming and seam allowances. (Fig. 10-10)

Fig. 10-10 Make a speedy gift bag out of scraps or remnants.

2. Finish the top of the bag with a double hem or any other quick method, such as pinking or serge-finishing.

3. Fold the bag right sides together with the finished edge at the top. Fold a piece of ribbon in half and sandwich it between the two layers with the folded end near the bag top about 1/4" past the cut edges. **Note:** The length of ribbon needed and the distance it is positioned from the bag top will depend on the size of the bag. When in doubt, use a longer ribbon and trim any excess later. Pinch in the fabric near the top to determine where the ribbon placement will look best.

4. Sew or serge the side and bottom of the bag using 1/4" seam allowances and catching the folded ribbon end in the stitching. Be careful not to stitch over any other part of the ribbon. Turn the bag right side out.

Serger tip: Decoratively finish gift bags with seams-out serging. Cut a rectangle twice the bag height by the bag width plus 1/2". Serge-finish the short ends and fold the rectangle in half with wrong sides together. Serge-finish the ribbon with matching thread and position it down from the top edge on one side. Serge-finish both sides of the bag, catching the ribbon in the stitching. (Fig. 10-11)

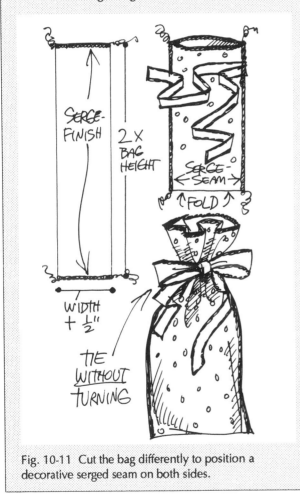

Fig. 10-11 Cut the bag differently to position a decorative serged seam on both sides.

♦ Make a drawstring pouch to wrap a small gift in style. If desired, use a nontarnish flannel, available in most full-service fabric stores, on the inside of the pouch so it can double as a jewelry bag later.

1. Prepare the pouch fabric following the previous directions for circular fabric gift wrap (see Fig. 10-4).

2. Make a casing on the outside of the pouch using single-fold bias tape. Place the tape away from the circular edge where you want to position the drawstring. Steam liberally to shape it around the curves. Turn under 1/2" on both ends of the tape and butt them together. (Fig. 10-12)

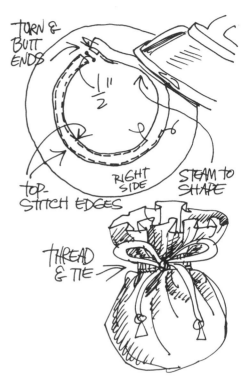

Fig. 10-12 Top-stitch bias tape to a circular fabric wrap to make a drawstring pouch.

3. Top-stitch along both folds of the tape, leaving the ends open for the drawstring. Thread a length of cording or ribbon through the casing and pull up the pouch.

♦ Wrap a larger gift in a fabric bag that can be used as a tote later.

1. Cut a fabric rectangle equal to twice the bag height plus 1" by the bag width plus 1/2". If desired, machine-embroider a name or motif on the right side.

2. Finish the short ends with a 1/4" double hem. (Fig. 10-13)

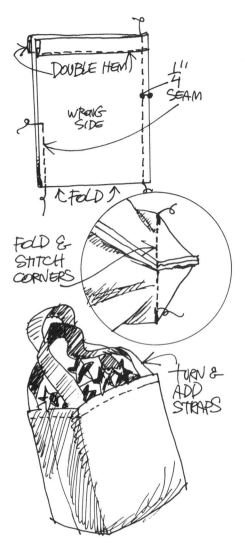

Fig. 10-13 Fabric bags are quick and reusable.

3. Fold the bag right sides together and seam both sides using 1/4" allowances. Then fold the lower corners to points with the seam in the middle. Straight-stitch across the seams at a right angle to box the bottom of the bag. Stitch close to the point for a narrower bottom or further away for a wider one.

4. Cut webbing handles and top-stitch them to the inside top edges of the bag.

Speedy Wrapping Accessories

Hunt through your sewing supplies and notions for decorative items that will turn a plain package into a memorable one. In many cases, the package accessory can be used by the recipient and becomes an extra gift.

Floral sprays, purchased appliqués, lace motifs, frogs, buttons, bead strands, and jingle bells all are potential wrapping embellishments. For fellow sewing enthusiasts, attach decorative notions to the outside of the package. Small scissors, a pretty needle case, a thimble in a holder, and a small pincushion are all possibilities.

When possible, use a length of matching ribbon to tie the accessory to the package, knotting the ends under the bow. Glue is an option only if the accessory will not be reused. An alternative is to use small circles or squares of sticky-back *Velcro* to hold the item in place.

If you can spare the time, put your sewing machine and creative skills to work making a special accessory:

♦ Construct tiny potpourri bags using the directions for either the flat or circular bag explained previously. Add a strip of lace or eyelet to the top edge for a decorative touch. Use chiffon or layer tulle and lace fabric for see-through bags. (Fig. 10-14)

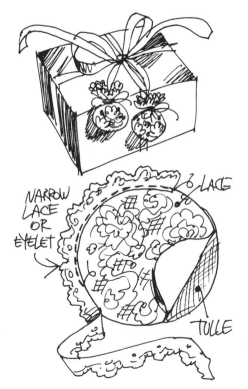

Fig. 10-14 The diameter of the finished circle should measure approximately 6" for a small package.

♦ Although you can make rosettes by gathering one long edge of a fabric strip, speed up the process by using lightweight beading or floral wire:

1. Cut a 10" by 1" strip of nonravelly fabric and round the corners on one long edge. (For a decorative effect and more stability, you may want to pink the long rounded edge.) (Fig. 10-15)

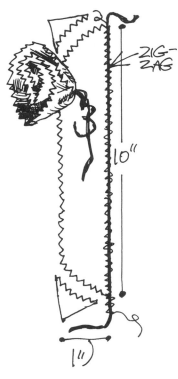

Fig. 10-15 Make quick rosettes using lightweight wire.

Serger tip: Highlight the rounded rosette edges using a rolled edge or narrow balanced stitch and decorative thread.

2. Using a wide stitch, zigzag or serge over a wire strand on the long straight edge. Leave 3" wire tails on each end.

3. Roll the fabric into a rosette and twist the wire tails to keep it secure. Then wrap the wire around the ribbon or bow on the package.

♦ Create gift tags for any occasion by machine-embroidering on fabric:

1. Stabilize the fabric with tear-away stabilizer or paper. Machine-embroider the to and from names and a short message on a single layer of solid-color fabric. Remove the stabilizer.

2. Fuse a second layer of fabric wrong sides together with the embroidered fabric using fusible transfer web. (Fig. 10-16)

Fig. 10-16 Embroider several tags on a larger piece of fabric before fusing and cutting them out.

3. Cut out a small square or rectangular tag with the embroidered greeting centered in the middle. Use pinking shears or decorative serge-finishing to add interest to the edges, if desired.

4. Use a paper punch to make a hole on one end of the tag for threading a ribbon to attach the tag to the gift package.

Glossary of Sewing Terms

All-purpose thread–Usually a cotton-covered polyester or 100% polyester thread wound parallel on conventional spools.

Appliqué–Attaching a separate piece (or pieces) of fabric, usually in a decorative shape, to a project. Fusible transfer web is often used to position an appliqué before top-stitching or fabric painting the edges to the project fabric.

Back-stitch–Taking several stitches forward and back over the beginning or end of a seam to prevent it from pulling apart.

Balanced stitch–Serged stitching in which the upper- and lower-looper thread tensions are balanced so the threads meet at the edge of the fabric, forming interlocking loops.

Binding (one-step)–A ribbon folded lengthwise, positioned over the fabric edge, and top-stitched to catch both ribbon edges.

Binding (two-step)–A strip of fabric (usually bias) sewn to an edge, then wrapped around it and secured to hide the seam and the raw edge.

Butt–To put the ends of a trim or casing against each other without overlapping.

Decorative machine stitching–Usually any sewing-machine stitches other than straight-stitching or zigzagging, although those too can be decorative when using a contrasting thread.

Decorative serging–Any serged stitching on the outside of a garment or project that enhances design detail, usually using a decorative thread.

Decorative thread–Any thread other than all-purpose or serger thread, although even a contrasting color of these threads is technically considered decorative. Our favorite decorative threads include buttonhole twist, woolly nylon, rayon, pearl cotton, crochet thread, machine-embroidery, and metallic.

Edge-stitch–A medium-length (10 to 12 stitches/inch) straight-stitch applied near an edge of the project.

Fabric paint–Paint sold in applicator-tip bottles that is specifically made for decorating fabric. All brands are washable and some are dry-cleanable.

Filler cord–Crochet thread, pearl cotton, buttonhole twist, or other heavy thread that raises the stitches made over it. Filler cord is also used as a gathering drawstring when zigzagged or serged over without stitching into it.

Flatlock–A serged stitch in which the needle thread is loose enough so the stitches flatten out on top of the fabric, forming decorative loops when the fabric is pulled apart. The underside will show a ladder effect of evenly spaced double parallel stitches. Used for both seaming and decorative stitching on a folded edge.

Grain–The direction of the fabric. Crosswise grain runs from selvage to selvage. Lengthwise grain runs the length of the yardage. Bias grain is diagonal to the other two. Fabric usually stretches more in the crosswise direction than in the lengthwise direction.

Heavy thread–Crochet thread, pearl cotton, or buttonhole twist used for serge-gathering or filler cord in piping or raised stitching.

Machine-baste–A long (6 to 8 stitches/inch) straight-stitch on a sewing machine used for holding two layers in position or for gathering.

Machine-embroider–Decorating the project fabric with either programmed machine stitches or free-machine embroidery designs.

Matching thread–Thread the same color as (or that blends as well as possible with) the project fabric.

Medium-length serged stitch–A stitch length of about 3mm.

Medium-width serged stitch–A stitch width of about 3.5mm.

Miter–A corner joint in which the folds are positioned at a 45-degree angle.

Monogram–Decorative initials stitched on a project using either programmed machine stitches or free-machine embroidery.

Narrow-width serged stitch–A stitch width of 2mm to 3mm. Used to serge a narrow seam or edge.

Piping–Fabric-covered cording inserted into a seamline with the covered cording exposed on the right side of the project and the allowances sandwiched between the fabric seam allowances.

Press-mark–To press a crease in the project fabric that is used as a marking for a later step or application.

Rolled edge (or rolled-edge stitch)–A serged stitch created by altering the tension so that the raw edge of the fabric rolls to the underside. A short stitch length creates an attractive satin-stitch edge.

Satin-stitch (satin-length)–A zigzagged or serged stitch short enough so the thread covers the entire fabric over which it is stitched.

Serge-finish–Most often a medium-length, medium-width, balanced 3- or 3/4-thread serged stitch used to finish the edge of one layer during the construction process.

Serger thread–Thread designed for serging, usually with the same fiber content as all-purpose thread but lighter in weight and crosswound on cones or tubes

so that it feeds easily during higher-speed serger sewing.

Serge-seam–Most often a wide, medium-length, balanced 3- or 3/4-thread serger stitch used to seam two layers together.

Short stitch–A .75mm to 2mm stitch length.

Stitch-in-the-ditch–Stitching directly on top of a previous seamline to secure another layer positioned on the underside. Often used for nearly invisible stitching when applying a binding to an edge.

Straight-stitch–A medium-length (10 to 12 stitches/inch) straight stitch on a sewing machine.

Top-stitch–A sewing-machine stitch (usually a straight-stitch or zigzag) used to attach one layer of fabric or trim to the project fabric. Top-stitching is also used to secure hems and other fabric layers anywhere away from the project edge.

Wide serged stitch–A 5mm to 9mm stitch width.

Zigzag stitch–A basic sewing-machine stitch with a back-and-forth motion forming a series of short, sharp angles.

Zipper yardage–Sold on a roll with separate zipper pulls. You can create any length of zipper by applying a pull and bar-tacking or seaming across the ends.

Mail-order Resources

We recommend that every sewing enthusiast develop a special relationship with his or her local dealers and retailers for convenient advice and inspiration plus the ease of coordinating purchases. However, when specialty items cannot be found locally or when a home-sewer lives several miles from a sewing retailer, mail-order specialists are a worthwhile option.

Authors' note: In today's volatile business climate, any mail-order source list will change frequently. Please send your comments on any out-of-business notifications or unsatisfactory service to Tammy Young, 2269 Chestnut, Suite 269, San Francisco, CA 94123.

Key to Abbreviations and Symbols

SASE = Self-addressed, stamped (first-class) envelope

L-SASE = Large SASE (2-oz. first-class postage)

* = refundable with order

= for information, brochure, or catalog

Recommended Resources

Aardvark Adventures, P.O. Box 2449, Dept. TY, Livermore, CA 94551, 510/443-2687. Books, beads, buttons, and bangles plus an unusual assortment of related products. Decorative thread, including metallics. $2*#.

Clotilde, Inc., 1909 S.W. First Ave., Ft. Lauderdale, FL 33315, 800/772-2891. Wide range of supplies, including acid-free tissue paper and *Ribbon Floss,* plus numerous other notions and supplies, books, and videos. Free#.

A Great Notion Sewing Supply, Ltd., 13847 17A Ave., White Rock, BC, Canada V4A 7H4, 604/538-2829. Hard-to-find sewing supplies. $1 U.S.#.

Home-Sew, Bethlehem, PA 18018. Sewing notions and a wide variety of trims. Free#.

Jehlor Fantasy Fabrics, 730 Andover Park West, Seattle, WA 98188, 206/575-8250. Baubles, bangles, and beads. $2.50#.

Madeira Marketing, Ltd., 600 E. 9th St., Michigan City, IN 46360, 219/873-1000. Popular decorative threads. SASE#.

Mill End Store, Box 82098, Portland, OR 97282-0098, 503/786-1234. Broad selection of fabrics, notions, trims, threads, and accessories. SASE#.

Nancy's Notions, Ltd., P.O. Box 683, Beaver Dam, WI 53916, 800/833-0690. Wide range of sewing notions and accessories, *Ribbon Floss,* threads and tools, interfacings and fabrics, books, and videos. Free#.

National Thread & Supply, 695 Red Oak Rd., Stockbridge, GA 30281, 800/847-1001, ext. 1688; in GA, 404/389-9115. Name-brand sewing supplies and notions. Free#.

Newark Dressmaker Supply, Dept. TY1, P.O. Box 20730, Lehigh Valley, PA 18002-0730, 215/837-7500. Sewing notions, trims, buttons, and decorative threads. Free#.

Sew-Art International, P.O. Box 550, Bountiful, UT 84011. Decorative threads, notions, and accessories. $2*#.

Sew/Fit Co., P.O. Box 397, Bedford Park, IL 60499, 800/547-4739. Sewing notions and accessories, cutting tables, cutting mats, special rulers, and T squares. Free#.

Sewing Emporium, 1079 Third Ave., #B, Chula Vista, CA 91910, 619/420-3490. Hard-to-find sewing and serging notions and parts, sewing-machine cabinets, custom-made machine accessories, and threads. $4.95*#.

The Sewing Place, 18770 Cox Ave., Saratoga, CA 95070. Sewing-machine and serger needles and feet plus books by Gale Grigg Hazen. Specify your brand and model when ordering machine accessories. L-SASE#.

Solo Slide Fasteners, Inc., P.O. Box 528, Stoughton, MA 02072, 800/343-9670. All types and lengths of zippers plus other selected notions. L-SASE#.

Speed Stitch, 3113-D Broadpoint Dr., Harbor Heights, FL 33983, 800/874-4115. Machine-art kits and supplies, including all-purpose, decorative, and specialty serging threads, books, and accessories. $3*#.

Treadleart, 25834 Narbonne Ave., Lomita, CA 90717, 800/327-4222 or 301/534-5122. Books, sewing supplies, notions, decorative threads, and creative inspiration. $3#.

YLI Corporation, 482 N. Freedom Blvd., Provo, UT 84601, 800/854-1932 or 801/377-3900. Decorative, specialty, and all-purpose threads, yarns, and ribbons. $2.50#.

Are you interested in a quarterly newsletter about creative uses of the sewing machine, serger, and knitting machine? Write to *Creative Machine Newsletter,* PO Box 2634-B, Menlo Park, CA 94026.

Other Books by the Authors

ABCs of Serging, Chilton Book Company, 1991, $16.95. The complete guide to serger sewing basics, by Tammy Young and Lori Bottom.

Distinctive Serger Gifts and Crafts, Chilton Book Company, 1989, $14.95. The first book with one-of-a-kind serger projects using ingenious methods and upscale ideas, by Naomi Baker and Tammy Young.

Innovative Serging, Chilton Book Company, 1989, $14.95. State-of-the-art techniques for overlock sewing, by Gail Brown and Tammy Young.

Innovative Sewing, Chilton Book Company, 1990, $14.95. The newest, best, and fastest sewing techniques, by Gail Brown and Tammy Young.

Know Your *baby lock,* Chilton Book Company, 1990, $16.95. Ornamental serging techniques for all *baby lock* serger models, by Naomi Baker and Tammy Young.

Know Your Pfaff *Hobbylock,* Chilton Book Company, 1991, $17.95. Ornamental serging techniques for all *Hobbylock* serger models, by Naomi Baker and Tammy Young.

Know Your Serger, Chilton Book Company, 1992, $16.95. Ornamental serging techniques and all-new projects for any serger brand, by Naomi Baker and Tammy Young.

Know Your White *Superlock,* Chilton Book Company, 1991, $16.95. Ornamental serging techniques for all *Superlock* serger models, by Naomi Baker and Tammy Young.

Serged Garments in Minutes, Chilton Book Company, 1992, $16.95. A complete guide to simple construction techniques, by Tammy Young and Naomi Baker.

Simply Serge Any Fabric, Chilton Book Company, 1990, $14.95. Tips and techniques for successfully serging all types of fabric, by Naomi Baker and Tammy Young.

Taming Decorative Serging, by Tammy Young, self-published 1991, $14.95. A step-by-step workbook teaching special techniques for glamorous decorative serging.

Taming Your First Serger, by Lori Bottom and Tammy Young 1989, $14.95. A hands-on guide to basic serging skills in an easy-to-use workbook format.

Look for these titles in your local stores, or write for a complete, up-to-date listing: Tammy Young, 2269 Chestnut, Suite 269, San Francisco, CA 94123. To order, add $3.50 per book to the listed price for shipping and handling.

Index

About the Authors

Naomi Baker is a nationally recognized sewing and serging authority who writes regularly for major industry publications and has coauthored seven previous Chilton books with Tammy Young. A home economics graduate of Iowa State University and a former extension agent, she worked for Stretch & Sew for ten years. She specializes in technique research and development and is well known for her dressmaking skills.

Naomi has a sewing consulting business, is a frequent guest on national television shows, and appears across the country at special workshops and conventions. She lives and works in Springfield, Oregon, with her husband and family, a huge fabric stash, and an enviable number of sergers and sewing machines.

Tammy Young is known for her creative ideas and techniques and for writing precise, detailed instructions. With a home economics degree from Oregon State University, she has an extensive background in the ready-to-wear fashion industry, as well as being a former extension agent and high school home economics teacher. Tammy has coauthored ten previous Chilton books.

Living and working in San Francisco's Marina District, Tammy founded and managed the *Sewing Update* and *Serger Update* newsletters before selling them in 1991. Now she enjoys working on creative projects and dreaming up ideas to try in her "spare time."